Go and Tell Redemp Story

The Autobiography of

Hector G Hall

Founder and Director, under God, of

The Mission to Mobile Homes

Boston, Lincolnshire, UK

2019

This book is dedicated to my Beloved Wife and Sweetheart, Ann Catherine Hall

Hector and Ann Hall

Published by Hector G. Hall
Boston,
England
September 2019

ISBN 978-1-5272-4845-8

The scripture quotations, paraphrases and references are taken from the Holy Bible, Authorized King James Version.

Printed and bound in the UK by
Book Printing UK, Peterborough

Foreword

It is my privilege to be able to recommend this short book, especially as other friends and colleagues who might have done so are now either unwell or in glory. Many years ago, at Quennevais Evangelical Church in Jersey, I met Hector Hall for the first time and heard him speaking about his work of visiting caravan sites and mobile home parks with the good news of the Gospel. Hector has persevered patiently in this good work, often ploughing a lonely furrow, but sometimes in partnership with fellow workers in different parts of the country or abroad.

When we later moved to Scotland, we met Hector again when he was visiting on nearby caravan parks. Hector has followed closely in the footsteps of the Saviour, the Son of Man who came to seek and to save the lost, and has felt this special call to those living outside the ordinary residential areas of our towns, people often overlooked by the churches.

Hector's gentle and winsome manner has opened many doors, and his great care for individual people is evident in all that he does. Like our Lord on earth, he is never in a rush and takes each person and their situation seriously. Conversations are followed up with earnest prayer for God to work in that person's life. Hector has sown the Word of God faithfully for a long time, and looks to the Lord of the harvest to give the increase and bring many sons and daughters to glory from the mobile homes of the land.

Hector has followed too the example of the apostle Paul, who tried by all means to save some, and has made constant use of booklets, tracts and Scripture portions, obtaining these in different languages to meet varying needs. He has preached in local churches, and sought in every way to tell the old, old story that is ever new — the story of Jesus and his love. Hector has been fully supported by his wife Ann, even through her times of ill health, and they have always been one in their prayers for this work.

May the reading of this wonderful account stir your heart to pray for the lost, and to be active where the Lord has set you in bearing witness to your faith in Jesus Christ. In a world that is heading in completely the wrong direction, Hector and those like him will always be going against the stream; but the Holy Spirit within God's people is the constant pledge and reminder that they are headed in the right direction, to safety and glory and eternal life. After all, what can compare with the joy of telling about one's Saviour, and seeing another heart opened like Lydia's? What actually matters in life, except the treasure laid up in heaven? May our values not be those of this world, but of our Saviour; and may our greatest joy be in faithfully serving him.

John R. de la Haye

Dingwall, Ross-shire

(February 2019)

Commendation

Go and Tell Redemption's Story
by Hector Hall

The story of the Mission to Mobile Homes is set in the wider context of the Author's life story from his early days during WW2, his coming to faith in Christ as a young teenager, his marriage to Ann and subsequent addition of two daughters, and his various preparative steps towards his eventual life of focused evangelistic ministry. The Author was led to identify mobile home owners and their families as a 'People Group', many of whom had had little or no contact with or awareness of the Good News of Jesus Christ, and it was to these people that Hector and his wife Ann devoted their time and energy. The book provides a fascinating and detailed overview of how the MMH developed both within the UK and internationally (Canada).

The book is informative as to people, places and dates. It draws upon a wide range of magazine articles, newsletters, personal correspondence, publicity notices as well as personal reminiscences. It is clear that the Halls were not alone but worked together with others in the team. Beyond mere information, the book is also inspiring because the reader cannot but be challenged by the consistent and tireless devotion of the Author over many years to share the Gospel meaningfully with mobile home owners. Along with the positives there were inevitable discouragements and there were many times when resources for living and ministering were low, and the Halls could only trust in God to provide, which He did. And this is the other reason why the book is inspiring: it testifies to the faithfulness and dependability of God; His love and trustworthiness in all circumstances, and the greatness of the Good News of Christ and His power to transform lives.

I trust that many will be blessed and challenged by this book.

Gordon Molyneux
(February 2019)

Acknowledgements

With thanks for the contributions made.

Fellow-workers who served with the Mission:

John and Margaret Bugg	Noel and Sandra Ramsey
George And Ann Stark	Adrian Underwood

Students from BELFAST BIBLE COLLEGE
who spent a Field Term with the Mission:

Ian Clarke	Paul Jamieson
Laura Sanlon	

Caravan Church Project: Lay Pastors

James Brownlee	Alex Marshall
John Norrie	

This book would not have been finished without the help of my good friend Nigel T. Barber, who has kindly computerised each chapter and given full support.

I am responsible for what is written.

With thanks to my kind friends John R. de la Haye for writing the FOREWORD, and Gordon Molyneux for writing the COMMENDATION.

The term 'Mobile Homes' is a misnomer, as many people live in them for many years as their permanent homes. A more popular name of recent times is 'Park Homes'.

This book is a TESTIMONY to the GREAT FAITHFULNESS of GOD, to His promises (Lamentations 3:23; 2 Peter 1:4) and to the GREAT SAVING GRACE of our LORD JESUS CHRIST (Hebrews 7:25), who can "Save to the uttermost". And, also is a Challenge to fellow-Christians to testify in the Holy Spirit's power what great things the Lord has done for them (see *1 Peter 3:15*).

All to God's praise and glory.

Beulah, 70 Eastwood Road, Boston, Lincolnshire PE21 0PL, UK

18th February 2019   **H.G.H.**

Go and Tell Redemption's Story

Contents

Go and Tell Redemption's Story

Introduction

The words of the title of this book are taken from Edward H. Bickersteth's challenging hymn *"For My Sake, and the Gospel's, GO and Tell Redemption's Story."* They sum up the essence of this book: to be obedient to the Great Commission of Christ (Matthew 28:19 and Mark 16:15) and tell men and women, boys and girls of Jesus' love:

That Jesus died for their sins upon Calvary's Cross as their substitute, shedding His precious blood to redeem them; was buried and gloriously rose from the dead on Easter Day, and appeared to the Disciples, and of His Second Advent. **That** they must repent of their sins and get right with God, **and that** they should live for His glory. This glorious message I have been telling, preaching and proclaiming for the past fifty-eight years.

Although this book is basically giving my life's story (and also a good part of my dear wife Ann's life story, too) and more particularly of Christ's saving grace extended to me: it also recognises the contributions of others who served with me in The Mission to Mobile Homes.

Of those who served full-time: Adrian Underwood, George and Anne Stark, Noel and Sandra Ramsey, and John and Margaret Bugg (John served notably for 12 years and was also a Council Member). Starting from the principle of *Acts 1:8* *"But ye shall receive power, after that the Holy Ghost is come upon you: and ye shall be witnesses unto Me both in Jerusalem, and in all Judaea, and in Samaria, and unto the uttermost part of the earth."*

Thus, the work of the Lord through The Mission to Mobile Homes spread, from that initial visit to the Mobile Home Park by the River Clyde (see Chapter 14):

1967 June – August: To people on Mobile Home Parks across CENTRAL SCOTLAND
1967 October onwards: To Northamptonshire and Bedfordshire, ENGLAND
1968 To SOUTH WALES
1970 To NORTHERN IRELAND
1980 To ONTARIO, CANADA.

And to many other parts of ENGLAND, too!

1 My Early Years at Nazeing

I was brought up in the small but beautiful village called Nazeing, nestling on the edge of the Lea Valley (also known as the Lee Valley) on the Essex side. Nazeing is eight miles from Epping, and two miles from Broxbourne, Hertfordshire – but more significantly eighteen miles north-northeast of London.

My parents Cyril and Rose Hall had moved there in 1938 with my sisters Rosemarie and Iris, my elder brother Cyril, and myself, just prior to the outbreak of the Second World War. My father was an accountant, a quiet man probably due to his hearing difficulties: he had also lost his left arm due to being run over by a horse-drawn bus at five years of age. He had received some hard knocks in his life, but was of a fighting spirit, believing that obstacles were there to be overcome. His elder brother Sydney was a Corporal in the Middlesex Regiment. My father often sat me on his knee when I was a little boy, as he sat in the armchair by the book-case in the front room, and told me how Sydney had died in Belgium in the First World War, and had lain for days on the battlefield – it was difficult to hold back tears.

Now Nazeing is a village with a strong Puritan connection, for John Eliot (c. 1604 – 1690), known as the "Apostle to the North American Indians", lived in Nazeing as a boy.

"His family arrived in Nazeing in 1607; Bennett Eliot had clear Puritan leanings. He was a thrifty, hard-working farmer and was determined to give John, the fifth child, the best available education. John went to Jesus College, Cambridge at the age of fifteen, already immersed in strong Puritan teaching, to pursue a B.A. Degree... He had a particular interest in Hebrew and Greek; all valuable assets for the life to which he would be called."

(Taken from *"Noncomformity in Nazeing – A History of the Congregational Church"*, authors Norman Bonnett and Paddy Hutchings, by their kind permission.)

I remember how, in my last year at Nazeing County Primary School, our headmaster Mr. Hills took us on a school outing to Cambridge University to see John Eliot's Bible there! As well as the Congregational Church, there was of course a Parish Church – "All Saints" – at the top of the village, of which more will be revealed later.

Some Memories of Childhood...

I have many happy memories of my childhood, although mixed with less happy ones due to the Second World War being on at that time. We were privileged to have a large garden, with me at four years of age pushing the lawn mower! Also, there was behind our garden an open field, then a fruit orchard in the middle, with a large open field at the bottom.

The Anglican Sunday School football team, managed by Mr. Martin, later played on this bottom field, after we had found a lime marker in the shed that previous owners had used to mark out their tennis court. Peter Daniels' father was a local builder, and he provided the wooden scaffolding poles that we adapted and used as goalposts and crossbar. (It looked like a Rugby Ground, because the uprights extended above the crossbar!) And Mr. Martin purchased black and amber football shirts (the same colours as Hull City Football club) – this was of course just after the war.

It was not unusual even in the war years to roam the Essex countryside behind our own field in what is now part of the Lea Valley Park. The land immediately behind our field had a slope to it on the west side, so that at the top you could see for miles, to the north and to the east. On the horizon on a clear, bright sunny day you could see the tops of buildings, for example factories, as far away as Welwyn Garden City. In my bright childhood imagination, I mistakenly thought the chimneys of the Welgar Shredded Wheat Factory were funnels of a large ship.

On this same hill in the historic winter of 1947, with its heavy snowfall we enjoyed tobogganing. People came from miles around with their sledges. I remember making my own wooden sledge that worked, not bad for a ten-year-old! The field had a natural slope, with a plateau to launch off, and two-thirds down a two-foot drop to send you on your way at great speed, but safely, as the field at the bottom was flat. The snow had been very deep – two to three feet at least. I didn't know then what the Prophet Job observed and wrote of as "The treasures of the snow" (*Job 38:22*), although I did take note of its purity when it first comes down from heaven. And its many beautiful designs.

Later the truth spoken of by the Prophet Isaiah came home to me:
Isaiah 1:18 "Come now, and let us reason together, saith the LORD, though your sins be as scarlet, they shall be as white as

2

snow." [*A.V.*]

The forgiveness and cleansing of the blood of Jesus makes us clean like the pure snow.

We had a large greenhouse, situated across almost the whole of the back garden, which had its own story to tell. The Lea Valley at that time was still famous for its Tomato industry. A Nurseryman from a nearby street wanted to use it, for food was short. He was doing well and making money on the black market. He asked my father what he was going to do with his greenhouse? "I will put tomato plants in a little later, when it is warmer, but I won't put on heating." The nurseryman replied, "You won't do any good!" Sadly, that man and his wife emigrated to South Africa to avoid trouble with the authorities. There they had a hard time: only his wife's dressmaking skills saved them.

My father on the other hand, in the goodness of God, would bring in – during the war years – trays of ripe tomatoes. He even supplied a local greengrocer with tomatoes! However, it was not to be all plain sailing – the terrible V2 rocket explosion (see Chapter 2) blew all the glass out of one side of the greenhouse and of the roof. My father cleared the broken glass in to one corner, put in a fresh lot of tomato plants in the cleared section, and we still had a harvest of juicy tomatoes! Mr. Hitler was not going to win. (Incidentally, the windows on the damaged roof were never repaired.).

My father had a client who had a shoe shop in Broxbourne High Road and he was able to get me one of the very first leather footballs available after the war. Inside was a rubber bladder that had to be blown up; and the outer tied like a pair of shoes. It was very rare at that time: so much so, that older boys of my brother Cyril's age were always wanting to borrow it to play down the road in Mr. Fowler's field. (Only a stone's throw from where the V2 rocket dropped.)

2 V2 Rocket Disaster from Nazi Germany

On Sunday 12th November 1944 at 11.32 am an event was to take place at St. Leonards Road, Nazeing, Essex that would literally shake the neighbourhood, destroy houses, and sadly leave ten dead and a number seriously injured. It had been, to start with, just like any other Sunday morning – except we were not in church. One moment all was quiet, then the V2 rocket struck – its speed, three times the speed of sound. Those in the Parish Church and the Congregational Chapel heard the explosion from a distance.

Two brothers, my school friends Billy and Dinkle King, were cutting sticks out of the hedge at the farm side of the field, just four or five feet from me. They were blasted by shrapnel from that explosion, were mortally wounded, and sadly died in the ambulance on the way to hospital. Cyril, my brother, and his friend Robin Pallet were up a tree – at a height level with the hedge – but amazingly they were not badly injured. They were however blown down out of the tree, and were terribly shaken.

Cyril later told me he couldn't get through to home, so half dazed he walked down to Pound Close, then had to come back along St. Leonards Road, past the rocket crater in the middle of the road, and the demolished Tatsfield Villas, in order to get home. In the explosion I personally had been blasted by shrapnel and had landed some twenty feet away from where I had been before.

My elder sister Rosemarie went looking for me and found me in the field with my clothes burnt black and later said that she "thought I was a goner". She later revealed that she had been upset because she had helped in carrying me to the ambulance, but was not allowed to accompany me to Hertford County Hospital. I was unconscious for a week, with a fractured skull, serious shrapnel wounds to my legs, and burns to my body. (Even today, 74 years later, there is still shrapnel across my chest, which shows up on X-ray photographs).

My sister Iris had been just coming down the stairs when the front door of our house blew in. It must have been quite a shock to her – she was eight, nearly nine years of age. My parents arranged for the Vicar of Hertford to come in to the Hospital and christen me, which he did the very next day, 13th November. This was because they mistakenly thought I would be saved from being eternally lost by being christened. God is merciful, and after a week I suddenly regained consciousness. It must have been a great trial to my loving parents and family.

When I came to in the hospital I looked across the Children's Ward, and there was my brother Cyril in one bed, and Freddie Sewell, who had been rescued from his damaged bungalow, in another. What were they doing there? What was *I* doing there? Then all of a sudden, I realised that bandages covered me, and that these bandages covered serious injuries, and with operations to follow – a lot for a seven-year-old to take in. My time in the hospital was from 12th of November till after Christmas 1944.

4

My family came in to see me, but visiting was very restricted in those days, so my father asked the Matron for extra visits.

Christmas 1944 was very memorable. I feigned being asleep on Christmas Eve as the nurses came around with presents, and put them at the bottom of my bed. On Christmas Day, doctors dressed up as *Rudolph the Red Nosed Reindeer*, and came around to every child on the ward. On the day I was transferred to St. Margaretsbury Convalescent Home, I came out on a trolley to the Ambulance, and snow was on the ground a couple of inches deep. I must have been in the Convalescent Home for at least two weeks.

This Convalescent Home was situated in beautiful grounds, and looked even prettier with the snowy scene. We walked through the building to the Dining Room at the back and one could see out into the garden where there was a giant Snowman. Recovery was slow but sure, and I did like the roasted potatoes they served! They also let me do a little light work, sweeping the floor.

Eventually they allowed me to go home, and as I travelled along St. Leonards Road the real effects of the rocket damage were very visible, and I was surprised to see that the houses had not yet been repaired. A few months' recovery was still needed, and a lot of schooling was lost. Each November 12th we are mindful of the families of the ten who lost their lives. There is a special 'Memorial' to those who died on that day in All Saints Church Yard, Betts Lane, Nazeing. After a Memorial Service there a little later, Rev. Sutherland, Vicar of Nazeing, said to me as he put his arm on my shoulder: "*God must have had a purpose in preserving your life.*" I believe that is true.

At this point I would like to pay tribute to the surgeons at Hertford County Hospital, who put me together again, and to the nurses who lovingly cared for me during the six weeks spent in hospital.

3   The Cadet Hut Sunday School

After the War, near the bottom of the same St. Leonards Road, a Sunday School was started in an Army Cadet Hut by Mrs. Beatrice Catton. She, together with her family, had been evacuated from the East End of London, due to the terrible German bombing. Iris, my sister, told me that a Sunday School was going to be commenced and asked me "Would you consider going?" My reply was, "I'll give it a try!" Well, she and I did attend. Mrs. Catton the Superintendent was a kindly lady who led it with grace, and after a suitable children's hymn of praise to God, prayer and Bible reading, we split up into half-a-dozen classes in different parts of the building.

Mr. Martin, a short, tubby man with a kindly touch taught us boys. He worked as a Receptionist at The Great Eastern Hotel, in Liverpool Street, London. He later started the Sunday School Football Team mentioned in Chapter 1, with yours truly as captain. As the saying goes, I was football crazy! One Sunday afternoon Mrs. Catton introduced the Reverend Sutherland, Vicar of Nazeing. He wore a thick dark overcoat and he had a broad smile. He urgently needed new members to strengthen his Church Choir at All Saints Church. I was quite willing and had a reasonable tenor voice: I would go if my parents were in agreement, and they were.

I cycled the mile and a half to Church, and often met my day-school beginners' class teacher, who used to smack me at the back of my legs with a ruler! It must have been needed! Such is the irony of life. On the positive side we did sing the hymn 'Now the Day is Over' in her class at the end of each School day. A few years later I attended Confirmation Classes with the Rev. H. Hawkins at the Anglican Church (Rev. Sutherland having been called home), but was not impressed that the other two young men told rude jokes while we waited for the Vicar to arrive. I was confirmed on 27th June 1951 at the age of fourteen years, but with no inward change such as conversion.

However, during the next two years God's Holy Spirit began to bring me under deep conviction of sin, but the more I tried to become a better person the more I failed miserably. No doubt the reading of God's Word each Sunday from the Old and New Testaments, the singing of Psalms and Hymns and the prayers started to move me. And sometimes an occasional preacher knew the Lord and faithfully proclaimed His Holy Word and Gospel.

Also, I had spent much time out in the open countryside enjoying and exploring the Creation in all its power and beauty. Therefore, it wasn't so difficult to believe in a Creator God, who created the World and universe in six days as *Genesis Chapters 1 and 2* intimate. However, when I left School at fifteen years of age and went to work I did temporarily drift away from church, as the majority of people in it seemed to be no different from those 'in the world'.

Hector's Conversion

Then on a particular Sunday evening in June 1953 the Holy Spirit drew me to attend church once again. Bishops, Canons and Vicars I had heard preach in the past but this evening it was a simple Lay Reader who conducted the service. His actual text cannot be remembered but the LORD very definitely suddenly spoke to me. The Holy Spirit revealed Christ to as the One who had lovingly died on the Cross for my sins, and shed His precious blood to make peace with God on my behalf. More than that, He was the LIVING CHRIST − not a dead Saviour but a LIVING SAVIOUR.

As I looked to Christ Crucified my sins were immediately forgiven, and I was born again of God's spirit. As I left Church I was a new creation (*2 Corinthians 5:17*). Even the natural Creation seemed to have a new beauty. As George Wade Robinson says in verse 2 of his hymn "Loved with Everlasting Love":

Heaven above is softer blue,
Earth around is sweeter green;
Something lives in every hue
Christless eyes have never seen:
Birds with gladder songs o'erflow,
Flowers with deeper beauties shine,
Since I know, as now I KNOW,
I am HIS and He is MINE.

When I arrived home, I told my mother: she said, "Hector's become religious!" "No", I said 'I've become a CHRISTIAN!" The Bible then became alive to me, and prayer a reality. A precious, real experience!

Next-door to our family lived Miss Ethel Willis, a retired Hospital matron, who was a Christian and prayed for my family and me. As a little boy I used to get the weeds out of her crazy paving with an old kitchen knife, and she used to give me pocket money and marzipan sweets! But more significantly she used to say, "I remember you in the morning and the evening." I believe her prayers were thus answered!

4 Some Adventures in The Essex Countryside

As a young lad of eight to eleven years I was very adventurous, almost at times a 'dare devil' − probably due to my three months inactivity in hospital and subsequent convalescence. To start with, my interest in ornithology meant that I then knew more about birds, their nests, the colours of their eggs, and where to find them, than I do now. And I had a good birds' egg collection, which would not be allowed today. I roamed and explored the countryside, often but not exclusively on my own.

I climbed right to the top of one of the big tall elm trees in Fowler's second field, where it literally waved in the wind, and I sang, "It's a long way to Tipperary!" at the top of my voice. It was a bit scary, because this would be fifty feet high at least. The downward slope of the field in front of the tree made it seem even steeper. It gave a lovely view of St Leonards Road and Tatsfield Avenue, and further afield. Don Newton, who was a few years older than I, and who then also lived in St. Leonards Road, later climbed one of those same Elm trees. Having got nowhere near the top, he sadly fell and broke his leg; he had to sit his 'Eleven Plus' exam in Hertford Hospital – and he passed!

Another thing I used to do in the winter was to walk on the ice covering ponds, of which there were a number in Nazeing: winters in those days were colder. This was dangerous to say the least. Sometimes you would be near the middle of a pond when all of a sudden you would hear the ice creak – as it appeared to be cracking. And you would instantly stop, and listen. Such warnings had to be heeded! On occasions like that I would very gently, very slowly retrace my steps, and walk off the pond. Young people – such activity is not to be recommended. Needless to say, GOD did preserve my life.

An unexploded shell …and an unusual swimming pool

In the top field opposite Tatsfield Avenue there was a blockhouse built to defend against the possible German invasion, and this side of the hedge across the field the army dug out the 'Tank Traps'. In these, water gathered to a depth of four feet in places, thus making an ideal swimming pool. The banks were made of clay that baked hard in the summer sun. Here I, with others, learnt to swim. In this same field I once located an unexploded shell and told the ARP man. Robin Pallet saw the Bomb Disposal men safely defuse it – but yours truly was not allowed to miss school…

Each year a collection was made for the 'Guy Fawkes' bonfire in our field behind the greenhouse. We made a Guy, too, for November the 5th – even in those days my sympathy lay with the Protestants! On one occasion, a 'Boy Scout Rouser' firework didn't go off – perhaps the touch-paper had got wet. So, I emptied the gunpowder onto a piece of paper on top of the coal shed, and lit it with a match. It exploded in my face, singing my eyebrows, and nearly blinding me! Needless to say, you don't do things like that again!

Nazeing County Primary School had three partitioned class rooms, and was situated at Bumble's Green – a good school, teaching the "Three 'R's" – **R**eading, w**R**iting and a**R**ithmetic. But they certainly didn't prepare us for later life in the way they do today. I was a slow learner in the early years, but had just been getting on my feet educationally when the rocket dropped. Then I lost a lot of schooling due to time in hospital with the many operations and the subsequent convalescence. I loved history and geography, and did quite well at maths.

Mr. Hills the headmaster as he was called in those days was a good man. He would on occasion get us to sit in a circle, and get each of us to read a few verses from a chapter of the Bible, usually from the Acts of the Apostles. However, I didn't win any school class prizes, but I *did* win a competition for the one who could collect the most pounds weight of Rose hips from the hedgerows. I collected over 20lbs, which was used for Rosehip syrup, providing vitamin C for babies.

King Harold Secondary Modern School in Waltham Abbey was a completely different scene! It was an urban school with good teachers, who had to deal with a few difficult youngsters among their pupils. I did particularly well at woodwork and had a wooden Stool and wooden Mirror Frame chosen to be put on display in Waltham Abbey Town Hall. My mother later found the stool very useful. There was of course good work by other pupils on display as well!

Tottenham Hotspur Football Club
It was a pleasure in my early teens to go with my brother Cyril to watch Tottenham Hotspur (the SPURS!) play football at White Hart Lane. We used to get the train from Broxbourne Station to travel on the Liverpool Street line, get off at Northumberland Park Station and walk up the road to the famous ground. People would appear on foot from everywhere, all going in the same direction. We would go through the turnstile in the 'Boys' Enclosure Stand' high up at the West End of the ground on the south side in the corner. It cost only 1/6d (one shilling and six pence) in the old money – 7½p in today's decimal currency! It was a great thrill to watch the two teams come out, and when they did a great cheer went up. Ronnie Burgess, a Welsh International and the Spurs Captain, was a fine left half. There isn't space to refer to all the players....

On one occasion when Cardiff City were the visitors a Cardiff fan ran on to the pitch and stamped a Leek into the ground of the Tottenham goal. It didn't make any difference, as Cardiff lost! Ted Ditchburn was I believe the Spurs goalkeeper, and he was too good for them. My only regret is that I didn't keep the Match Programmes; they would be of great value now. My father supported the Spurs, and Middlesex for County Cricket, whilst I supported the Spurs, and Essex for County Cricket. And being on the Cambridge railway line, it was a case of Cambridge University for the BOAT RACE.

Nazeing Minor Football Team

I wrote to the secretary of Nazeing Football Club regarding the need for a Minor (Youth) Team. They kindly considered my request, and they did form such a team, which ran for a few years. It's good to be a catalyst!

5   The Transforming Effects of The Gospel of Christ

When Christ saves sinners, He transforms their lives for the better. The Apostle Paul affirms this:

> *2 Corinthians 5:17* "If any man be in Christ, he is a new creature: old things are passed away; behold all things are become new."

The BIBLE came alive to me, and I started reading it daily – nobody told me to. Eventually I got in to the good habit of reading a portion (or even a whole chapter) from the Old Testament in the morning, meditating on the words and praying for the Holy Spirit to teach me. This was done from the beginning of Genesis to the end of Malachi. Likewise, in the evening I was reading the New Testament from the beginning of Matthew to the end of Revelation.

The advantage of this scheme of Bible reading meant the whole Bible was read – in other words the whole counsel of God was received. The Old Testament took two and a half years approximately, and the New Testament about a year and a half. So, in the course of the sixty-five years since my conversion, the Bible has been read through and meditated upon at least twenty-five times. What a wealth of wisdom! This does not of course include those passages of Holy Scripture read for the preparation of Messages (sermons) that run in to hundreds, or for personal study of Bible subjects. Needless to say, the Word of the Living God changed my inner thoughts and life-style. "In what ways?" you may ask.

Firstly, His love in my heart replaced any hate.

> *Romans 5:5* "The love of God is shed abroad in our hearts by the Holy Ghost which is given unto us."

Secondly, on occasions I used to use swear words. The Holy Spirit changed my vocabulary. In the early days after conversion, it took a little time to adjust to the new man that I was in Christ. If I did use a wrong word I knew the Holy Spirit was grieved, so my speech began to change for the better.

And, thirdly, my temper began to be under the control of the Holy Spirit, Christ's representative. My new desire was always to live for Christ and to please Him. As St. Paul says, "To be conformed to the image of Christ." T. O. Chisholm expressed it thus:

> *O to be like Thee, blessed Redeemer,*
> *This is my constant longing and prayer;*
> *Gladly I'll forfeit all of earth's treasures,*
> *Jesus, Thy perfect likeness to wear.*

Chorus

> *O, to be like Thee, O, to be like Thee,*
> *Blessed Redeemer, pure as Thou art;*
> *Come in Thy sweetness, come in Thy fullness:*
> *Stamp Thine own image deep on my heart.*   Amen!

My great new desire was to share the Gospel of Christ with others. There were, of course, times in my life in those early days as a Christian when I failed the Lord, and had to ask the Lord's forgiveness. (*1 John 1:9*).

Heavenly Experience

There were also wonderful times of prayer with the Lord, particularly before I went to bed, and, strange as it may seem, in the bathroom of all places. This was the only place where it was possible to shut one's self in with the Lord and not be disturbed (our toilet was separate from the bathroom). It can only be described as a 'Heavenly Experience' – the Holy Spirit glorified Jesus, and revealed Heavenly truths, like being in the "Third Heaven" (*2 Corinthians 12:2*). My mother must have become a little concerned on one or two occasions, for she called out on one such occasion "Hector, go to bed!", as I had been there some time.

Also, I used to love going over the fields and to be able to pray extemporary prayers aloud to God. To sing praises to God for His wonderful creation and wonderful redemption through the precious blood of the Lord Jesus, and to pray for the salvation of sinners. Later I practiced preaching to the cows. They don't have eternal souls, however – I hope that I didn't turn their milk sour!

My Very First Bible Study with Fellow-Believers

Shortly after my conversion to and by the Living Christ, two brothers Ron and Brian Ford who did worship at the Congregational Chapel in my home village of Nazeing, Essex, invited me to their home for a Bible Study. How they came to know of my new life in Christ I do not know, except that I did take the opportunity to express my newly found faith in Christ to former school friends.

(One such former school friend was Bob Welsh, whom I met one day on the top deck of the number 327 bus as I boarded it at Broxbourne Station. I sat down next to him at the front of the bus: I told him that I had come to a personal faith in Christ, and that He had wonderfully Saved me by His grace. He listened with real interest.

Years later I learned that he had sadly died quite young – he had not had good health – but his mother revealed to my mother that he had been reading the Bible. So, I hope to see Bob in Heaven!)

Now to return to Ron and Brian... It was very kind and thoughtful of them to invite me as a new convert for fellowship and Bible study. After sixty-five years, however, it is difficult to remember much detail. Their home in Middle Street lay back from the road, literally across the field (now filled with new houses) from the Congregational 'Chapel Hall' as it was known. At that time J. B. Phillips' "*Letters to Young Churches*" was popular Christian reading. I know we studied some passages from the Acts of the Apostles, so that would have been appropriate. Also, the British and Foreign Bible Society published a John Stirling A.V. Bible. It was the ever theologically reliable King James Version with line drawings, which on the whole were very helpful for a young believer such as me, particularly a road sign that told us that Jerusalem is five miles from Bethlehem. Also, the maps and drawings of Roman coins and of the Shepherd Seeking the Lost Sheep (*Luke 15:1-7*) were outstanding, and did not in any way detract from the truth of Holy Scripture. For a new-born Christian as already indicated, it was most helpful.

Ron and Brian were bright and sincere, Christ honouring young men, whom it was a privilege to know: their faith was real, and they accepted me as a fellow-believer. We had extemporary prayer together. This was of course all new to me, being used to the set prayers of my Anglican background. God's presence was real. As our Saviour said:
Matthew 18:20 "For where two or three are gathered together in My name, there am I in the midst of them."

Jesus was present, fellowship was good with fellow-believers and I cycled back home with joy. We must have had only two or at the most three of these meetings. Why it stopped at that number I don't know, it must have been solely due to circumstances on my part, as there was no disagreement between us. Perhaps it was because of my work, or more likely because the Lord had led me on to Hoddesdon Baptist Church – of which, more later.

Mrs. Paddy Hutchins of Nazeing Congregational Church revealed to me that Ron Ford had later been called to be a Minister of the Gospel, and was at that time living in Australia.

6 Finding My Spiritual Feet...
...during my time in secular employment

I left King Harold Secondary Modern School at Waltham Abbey at fifteen years of age, and went to work in a coachbuilder's factory at Ware, Hertfordshire. The wage was 35 shillings a week (£1-75p)! Getting to work meant rising at 6am to get the first Number 327 bus from Nazeing to Ware. The work was physically hard, dirty and sometimes dangerous, particularly working under coaches. However, this gave me valuable experience of how men work on a factory floor, and the disciplines attached. Men miss out on such experience that go straight from College into a pastorate or other Christian service.

I stuck at it from September to Christmas 1953, but realised it was not my niche. God must have something else for me to do. After a lot of prayer on my part, my father intervened by suggesting that I write to Major J. C. Robinson, who lived in our village but worked in the City of London, and whom I knew from being a choirboy. So, I wrote to Major Robinson and he arranged an interview with the Manager of the Travel Department of Hogg Robinson & Capel-Cure. They then offered me a job as a Messenger Boy. Not just any type of messenger, but a Continental Ticket Messenger!

It became my job to visit all the Continental rail-offices, which were mainly situated in London's West End. My tour of visits usually finished at the 'Continental Enquiry Office' at Victoria Station. There, I had to personally submit vouchers for tickets for destinations all over Europe e.g. for *The Golden Arrow* train service to Paris. It was very interesting work! If the tickets were urgently needed I had to wait while they were issued. This required perseverance, as the ticket offices would only immediately issue tickets they considered urgent, and my firm sometimes needed tickets dated a month or two in advance to send out to clients in Australia and New Zealand. Also, reservations were made for accompanied travel.

Reception Received at Railway Offices

I used to travel to these offices on the London Underground, taking the Circle Line from Liverpool Street to Victoria. Those Circle Line trains could be recognised by having only one light at the front. Herewith are some comments on the different rail offices and my reception at them!

The **French Railways** office in Piccadilly was on a corner opposite to Fortnum & Mason. We representatives of the Travel Agents had to go upstairs, where they were not very obliging to say the least.

The C.I.T. **Italian Railways** were in Charles the Second Street. They were of typical Latin temperament, but were nonetheless helpful and friendly. As were the **Swedish Railways** staff, who couldn't have been more helpful, a most friendly people.

The Swiss National Tourist Office dealt with the **Swiss Railway** tickets, and was located in the Strand near Charing Cross. We went in by the back entrance to the building – across the road was St. Martin-in-the-Fields Church. They were quieter in temperament but most helpful and very reliable.

The **Austrian State Tourist Office** issued rail-tickets for travel in that country, and was visited only occasionally. When you opened the door in to the inner room, it was as if you entered the 'Austrian Tyrol'! There was a deep valley in the middle of the room with beautiful hills on either side – a really colourful 3D effect: a taste of Austria!

In the Travel Department at Hogg Robinson there were a few fellow-Christians, who were a challenge and an encouragement to me. Malcolm Cross, who job I took over, introduced me to Oswald J. Smith's books, *"Revival We Need"*, *"The Enduement of Power"* etc. They were a real blessing to me. O. J. Smith was the founder, under God, of *The Peoples' Church*, Toronto. (Many, many years later it was my privilege to speak at that church at a mid-week meeting on the work of **The Mission to Mobile Homes**, arranged by Dr. John Moore, who was acting moderator for that church at that time. There were about two hundred people present.)

Other Christians in the Travel Department were Bill East of the

European section and Harry Ibbotson of the Far Eastern section. Harry was something of a humourist and was loved by all. Like many firms in the City of London, it had its own Christian Fellowship, which met in the evening and was supported by Christians from other departments, these meetings being held in the Staff Restaurant in London Wall. At one point I received more spiritual help at work, than I did at Church. But change was soon to come...

Hoddesdon Baptist Church

On the home-church front I was receiving no spiritual food. The Rev. Sutherland, who was a real Christian, had died a few years earlier and the next Vicar didn't have much idea. By November 1953 I could stand it no longer, so after prayer a visit was made to Hoddesdon Methodist Church. It was a little better, but not quite what I needed. Then one Sunday God led me to Hoddesdon Baptist Church (H.B.C.), on the corner of Essex Road. The service was spiritual, the pastor Rev. Lionel Jupp gave a lively biblical message, and the people were warm hearted. On letting the Vicar at Nazeing know of my desire to change church, he had no real answer.

The **Young People's Fellowship** at H.B.C. was a great help to me. Gordon Cooper and Mike Wilbourne were then the leaders. We had a happy balance of weekly sporting activity and spiritual biblical teaching, and a helpful talk monthly by the Pastor. There was also a Summer Camp – under canvas – on a farm at Melbourne, Cambridgeshire. The fellowship was great, and much appreciated. In my non-Christian days, I was to be found at the Cinema on Saturday evenings, but the Holy Spirit convicted me after my conversion to attend the Saturday night Prayer Meeting at H.B.C.

A Witness Team led by Mrs. Jessie Weir gave me the opportunity to give a message from the Bible at Emmanuel Mission, at Bengeo, Hertford. Others taking part were Peter Assheton, Ralph Long, Jean Nicholls (later Mrs. Long), and Elva and Gavin Weir. John and Rhoda Dopson warmly welcomed us. At this time too, Gordon Cooper, a deacon as well as Y.P.F. Leader, very kindly took me out with him to lead services at village Congregational Churches – at Hertford Heath where there was a blind pianist, and you had to announce the last verse of each hymn, and at Stanstead Abbotts. There I would give a testimony, and preach, and thus gain useful experience of Christian ministry.

A change in my employment situation led me, in God's will, to work locally as a coal salesman with Coote & Warren at Broxbourne. Thereby

I gained experience in door-to-door work, meeting people in their own homes and witnessing to Christ as opportunity presented itself. Thus, also seeing something of the other side of life. This was all part of God's preparation for future ministry with the London City Mission (L.C.M.), the Railway Mission (R.M.) – and The Mission to Mobile Homes (M.M.H.).

Later the Lord spoke to me about Believer's Baptism, and I was baptized in obedience to Christ, aged 19 years. My sister Rosemarie was the only one of my family to attend the service. Then the Lord began to challenge me with regard to full-time Christian service, through a message given by Pastor Jupp and the verse *Joshua 14:8*:
"But I WHOLLY followed the LORD my God."

I was determined to be like Caleb – out and out – wholly living for CHRIST'S GLORY.

7   Crime – and a Prison Visit

Matthew 25:36b "I was in prison, and ye came unto me"

Whilst working as a Coal Salesman at Coote & Warren's Office by the side of the New River at Broxbourne, I called each week on people who, as was a practise in the late 1950s, paid for their coal, coke or anthracite by 50 pence (10 shilling) or £1 instalments. They each had their own Payment Book, similar to those that Insurance Agents used. When sufficient money had been paid in, a ton of coal would be delivered. If the people were out at delivery time, they would leave their money wrapped up with the payment book in many strange places!

I had my eyes opened as to how the other half of England lived. This was mainly in the Hoddesdon, Rye Park / Rye House urban area of Hertfordshire. I came of course from just over the county border at Nazeing in rural Essex. Incidentally, it was part of God's preparation for future Christian ministry – the Lord knows "the end from the beginning" (*Isaiah 46:10*). The son of one of my coal customers had got into trouble with the law – after over sixty years I cannot remember the exact details. His mother was naturally greatly concerned for him, and my concern to reach him with the Gospel of the grace of God meant a trip one Saturday morning to the Boy's Wing of Wormwood Scrubs Prison in London. This was my first ever visit to such an institution. Nowadays it is solely a women's prison.

On arrival there we were put into a kind of waiting room, after we had given our personal details. There were families of prisoners all waiting to see their loved-ones. Then suddenly my name was called and I went to meet the young fellow; he was about 16 years of age and unknown to me personally. It wasn't an easy experience as we all had to speak to the person through a grill and in a dull room, and we couldn't shake hands. Also, his particular interests were unknown to me. However, I tried to make conversation, to be friendly, and to tell him of God's love for him in Christ. I gave him a John's Gospel and a tract, and told him of his mother's love and concern.

A Great Deliverance

It was during this period as a Coal Salesman working in the Hoddesdon, Rye Park and Broxbourne area that I was to go through the traumatic experience of being attacked. One morning, whilst on my Raleigh cycle and paying calls in Rye Park, I noticed two men in a van draw up quite near me, but I didn't think anything more about it. A good lunch was had, as usual, at a restaurant opposite the Clock Tower in Hoddesdon, after which I cycled down to St. Augustine's Drive, at Broxbourne. I was reading the black Order Book as I slowly walked up the path to the front door of a bungalow, when all of a sudden two men appeared as from nowhere, knocked me down, and stole £49 from my inside pocket. They quickly sped back to their van, but having my biro still in my hand I quickly took down the vehicle registration number from the number plate. As I did so, one of the men got out of the van and turned the ends of the number plate: too late – I already had the number! Then I quickly crossed to Broxbourne Parade and went into one of the shops and telephoned the police.

When they came they found a cast iron builder's chisel on the ground. It is providential that they had caught me completely by surprise or I might have defended myself, and been hit on the head by such an object and not be here now. Thank God for His preserving mercies! These men were later caught and were given two-year prison sentences for robbery with violence. It was a front-page story in the *Hertfordshire Mercury*. Later, while I was at Bible College in Glasgow, I had to return home for a prisoner identification parade at Cheshunt County Court.

This experience affected my nerves for the next year or two. However, life went on – there was no trauma counselling in those days – you were soon 'back on the job'. Like remounting a horse after a fall…

8   First Impressions of B.T.I. Glasgow.

A week or ten days before my departure in September 1958 to study at the Bible Training Institute (B.T.I.) in Glasgow, Scotland, I sent my trunk on ahead. There I was to do a two-year Theological Course for the college Diploma.

How did I hear of B.T.I.?

In 1958 *"The LIFE of FAITH"* – a Christian newspaper – had a series of helpful articles on the Synoptic Gospels (Matthew, Mark and Luke) by the Rev. Andrew MacBeath, M.A. B.D., the Principal of B.T.I. This drew my attention to this missionary training college. After a lot of prayer and serious thought, and with the support of my home church, my application was made and I was accepted to commence studies in the term beginning in September 1958. A miracle indeed, as I had no educational qualifications!

My pastor, Rev. Lionel Jupp, and the Deacons at Hoddesdon Baptist Church, my home Church, had fully supported my application to the Bible Training Institute, which had come into being to train working men for Christian service following the Moody and Sankey Missions to Scotland. Prior to entering B.T.I. my education had been very minimal, since I had lost a lot of impetus due to the time lost in hospital at seven years of age whilst undergoing operations following injuries from the V2 Rocket explosion. But I was keen to read every piece of Christian literature. As Paul the Apostle says, "Be ye transformed by the renewing of your mind." (*Romans 12:2*) Thus I was very keen to learn and become an effective servant of God, and was ready and obedient to do His will.

My father, although not a Christian, was supportive and he gave me money to get a meal on the train (the Royal Scot?) from London Euston up to Glasgow. I had never been away from home for an extended period before. Many of my contemporaries had done National Service in the Forces, but I had missed this on medical grounds. After seven and a half or eight hours of travel we arrived at the bustling, impressive Glasgow Central Station. Fortunately, B.T.I. was only a street away in Bothwell Street!

The Gothic architectural style of the B.T.I. building was impressive, being on the corner of Bothwell Street and West Campbell Street, right in the centre of the City. You couldn't miss it, on the right-hand side, with the Christian Institute next door and next to that was the Y.M.C.A. There was a bustle of students in the entrance lobby, the office staff were welcoming and I was given a room on the second floor looking out onto West Campbell Street. We all had individual rooms, which I appreciated, and use of the communal washing facilities. There was a laundry at the very top of the building, too.

I instantly felt at home, although at times my ears had yet to get used to the broad Scottish dialect. No doubt it was the same in reverse! The men occupied one side of the building with the women on the other. Ne'er the twain shall meet! Not quite, because we did, however, all meet and mix at the Dining Room situated on the lower ground floor (at one time, there had been separate dining rooms). Meals were basically good, although too much savoury rice for my liking (spicy?) – obviously preparing students who would go to serve overseas, to India and the Far East. Alas, there was no Essex Rice Pudding!

The Lecture Hall was a large oblong room, with desks sloping down to the front. Men sat on the left-hand side, and women on the right-hand side, with the middle section half and half. There were at that time some 140 to 160 Students. We had an excellent Library, and recreation was on Tuesday afternoon.

We went to Bellahouston Park for football – some played hockey – boarding a tram outside the doors of B.T.I., going all the way to the Park. In one game with the W.E.C. (Worldwide Evangelisation Crusade) College I was put on the left wing and scored two goals with inswinger corners. David Beckham would have been proud of such! The W.E.C. supporters came with rattles etc. but usually lost: however, they won the honours for enthusiasm. Mr. MacBeath usually attended these inter-college games. The Women Students were very good. Many of them were qualified nurses, called of God to the foreign field.

Morning Worship was, I think, at 7.30am in the Lecture Hall, and was usually taken by each student in turn. On a Sunday a member of Faculty took the service, and at this service each student had to quote a text of scripture that had been a blessing to them during the week. In the first (Welcome) Meeting we each had to give our testimony – in about four minutes – of how we had come to know the Lord. That was a great and thrilling experience to hear, first hand, how the living God had worked in the hearts of such a variety of different people of different nationalities. It was a wonderful way of getting to know one's fellow students. The principal Rev. Andrew MacBeath chaired this meeting.

The first Lecture of the day began at 9.05am. In my second year I resided in the Y.M.C.A., I think in Room 189. Keith Ranger (Cambridge University and O.M.F.) played his accordion as Roy Carter and I enjoyed singing a favourite hymn or two from the '*Redemption Hymnal*' (or was it Sankey's '*Sacred Songs*'?). Then the B.T.I. siren would go off and we would quickly descend the stairs to arrive in time in the Lecture Hall next door!

The second Lecture of the morning was given by Rev. (later Doctor) Geoffrey Grogan M.Th. He lectured us in Systematic Theology, and years later became Principal of B.T.I. He was a big built man, and became known as the 'Gentle Giant'. He had the great gift of giving notes that were clear, logical – and of course biblical – easy to follow and to take down. One of the first doctrines he covered was "*The Finished Work of Christ*". He seemed to cover the Cross and The Atoning Work of Christ from every relevant book of the Bible, so we had a comprehensive grasp of this wonderful central doctrine.

My first contact with Mr. MacBeath's Bible teaching had been through articles in "*The Life of Faith*", which was edited by former B.T.I. student, Rev, H. F. Stevenson. And so, at B.T.I. Mr. MacBeath majored on the Bible, book by book. He encouraged us to read right through a book like Genesis in order to get what he called 'A Panoramic View'. We were to look out for reoccurring phrases, themes and words. We were of course dependent on the Holy Spirit to teach us. He was affectionately known as the 'Wee Man', as he was small of stature physically speaking but a man of great experience having been a missionary in Congo. He had experienced 'Revival', and had lectured at the Toronto Bible College (later Ontario Bible College). He was a Godly man of worldwide vision, with a winsome personality.

We used the Keswick Hymnbook with such hymns as were not universally used at that time by the Churches, but which are now in most modern hymnbooks. Hymns like '*Take time to be HOLY, Speak oft with Thy Lord...*' by William Dunn Longstaff. Mr. MacBeath always stressed a slight modification, '*Take time to BEHOLD HIM*' – that is the way to *become* Holy! Another one was '*Seek ye first, not earthly pleasure...*' by Georgiana Mary Taylor: God **must** always come first in your life.

> *Matthew 6:33* "Seek ye first the Kingdom of God, and His righteousness".

One of the joys of Bible College life was the fellowship of fellow-students. We had quite a few candidates from O.M.F. (formerly the

China Inland Mission). They were men and women of the finest calibre, having previously studied at Cambridge and Oxford Universities. Being from the East of England and a supporter of Cambridge on Boat Race day I am a little biased towards Cambridge!

One of my favourite visiting Lecturers was Dr. Arthur Fawcett, Minister of Johnstone High Kirk (Church of Scotland) who lectured in Church History. He made the subject come alive, and had a great sense of humour. We started with *THE REFORMATION in GERMANY* under Martin Luther, which was very well received. His method was to dictate notes, and in between he made his lively comments that filled out the subject and made it so much more interesting.

For our homework, we had not only to read up on the subject, but also to write an essay of 5,000 words on "*THE SCOTTISH REFORMATION*". This too I found most enlightening – there were Bishops of ten years of age! No wonder there was a more thorough reformation 'North of Border'. Dr. Fawcett also wrote a book on "*The Cambuslang Revival*", published by Banner of Truth. Dr. Grogan set us to write a Thesis of 10,000 words on Christology, the doctrine of the *PERSON of CHRIST*. This work was to be done in the Summer Vacation of 1959. Here I will let you in to a little secret! I had a small Imperial typewriter and with it typed out the Thesis during the summer vacation, handing it in upon my return to B.T.I. in September 1959.

For some reason I never received it back, marked. Why not? The other students received their marked Theses. I had unfortunately typed my name in small print at the end, as I was academically very shy. I thought that Dr. Grogan was very busy and had not finished marking it, and so I didn't want to pressurise him. But as time went on it was never returned. I don't blame Dr. Grogan; he was a lovely Christian man.

And so God gave me grace to complete the regular College examinations and essays with reasonable marks.

9   Unexpected Romance ! !

In my second year at B.T.I. I was allocated to speak to the Young People at Knightswood Baptist Church, Glasgow. They were a fine, lively and keen group of young people, and it went well. Then, when it was their Church Anniversary, Dr. Ernest Kevan of London Bible College was to be their Guest Speaker, so Ian Briggs, Roger Beresford and I attended this memorable Saturday afternoon meeting, me not realising its future significance.

It was there providentially that I met a certain Miss Ann Creighton who came over to speak to me, obviously recognising me from the earlier Y.P. meeting. (Although at that meeting another young lady had caught my attention – confession is good for the soul!). Ann's father at that time was Scottish Organizing Secretary for the Lord's Day Observance Society (L.D.O.S.), and Ann's mum invited us B.T.I. students back for supper – the Scots are good at hospitality.

Later we received an invitation to Ann's 21st Birthday Party at the Victory Club. It was a beautiful evening inside at the Party, but outside it was foggy – one of those real 'smogs' that we used to get before the Clean Air Act. In those days Boots the Chemist had a shop on the corner of Union Street and Argyll Street, and a day or two before the party Roger, Ian and I visited it to get Ann a 21st birthday present. Ian and Roger couldn't decide what to get Ann, but on the way up the escalator I noticed a lovely Vernon Ward picture of '*Land's End*'. She would like that I said, and later that picture was to hang in our dining room.

Things move quickly – that is, in matters of the heart. Ann had looked resplendent in her beautiful blue dress with her red rose on her 21st. She won my heart. After much prayer I decided to invite Ann to the B.T.I. Missionary Meeting. It took courage, since a large number of other B.T.I. students would of course be present. I suggested that she met me at *Wendy's Tea Shop* on the corner of Sauchiehall Street for a meal before going to the evening meeting.

In my letter to Ann a way of escape was given (in case I had misread the signals?) – she could bring a friend – but thankfully she did not. So, it was that a few days later a letter arrived from Ann, accepting my invitation. Her sister Joy on hearing of my letter and invitation had said to Ann, "What, that Englishman?" – all is forgiven, Joy! Ann duly arrived at Wendy's Tea Shop, and we found that we had so much in common. How wonderful of the Lord to bring us together. We enjoyed each other's company on that day, and have done so ever since.

> *Proverbs 18:22* "Whoso findeth a wife findeth a good thing, and obtaineth favour of the LORD."

However, marriage is a wonderful partnership in the Lord between one man and one woman, who love one another. As the Apostle Paul says:

> *2 Corinthians 6:14* "Be ye not unequally yoked together with

unbelievers."

We thank God we have been happily married for over 50 years. For further reading see *Ephesians 5:22-33*.

Ann on her part had prayed for a young man of similar Evangelical beliefs and convictions, who would proverbially be tall, dark and handsome: whether that was a true description of me at that time is not for me to say! But the Lord does delight to answer the specific requests that His children make in faith, if it is in accordance with His perfect will for that person's life.

> *Psalm 37:4* "Delight thyself also in the LORD; and He shall give thee the desires of thine heart."

Needless to say, I saw Ann home after the Missionary meeting, and even kissed her '*Good night*', then returned to the College with my heart in a real flutter! Ann, like me, loved the Lord, and had a sincere desire to serve the Lord.

Courtship and Marriage

As you might expect, many visits were made to Ann's home in the weeks that followed as our love deepened, and after saying '*Good night*' to Ann outside her home in Selbourne Road, her younger brother thought it amusing to put the milk bottles out at that critical moment! As you might also expect I got to know not only Ann, but also her family very well. William and Helen Creighton, her Dad and Mum, were most kind and gracious, and her brothers Angus and Sam and her sisters Joy and Evangeline warmly accepted me, and I felt very much at home. A truly Christian home is a wonderful blessing. We did our courtship in the different Parks of Glasgow, and the first Esquire House, a Coffee Shop at Anniesland, was a favourite place.

Ann's parents, who had served as missionaries in Peru and Argentina with the Irish Baptist Foreign Mission, knew B.T.I. Principal MacBeath very well. He and Rev. J. J. Johnston, Ann's pastor, conducted our Wedding Service at Knightswood Baptist Church on 16th June 1962 – a special day, much to be remembered. Ann's twin sisters Joy and Evangeline were charming bridesmaids, and Ann was the shy but beautiful bride.

I, the bridegroom, was kindly given hospitality at the Johnston's manse, as was Peter Assheton, our Best Man. However, as I turned in for the night I got an unexpected surprise. Underneath the bottom of the bedcovers were a variety of saucepans and cooking utensils! So much for a quiet night before a most important day. All to the delight of our hosts and of Peter!

Honeymoon Destination - Unknown?

Don't get excited.

Our 'Best Man', dear Peter Assheton, told us before the wedding that he had booked 'Bed & Breakfast' at a Guest House at Keswick in the Lake District, half way back from Scotland to his home in Hoddesdon, Hertfordshire. The only difficulty was that we had booked our Honeymoon accommodation at a Guest House in – guess it? – Keswick, the same town. So, we couldn't tell him, or more importantly Ann's parents or family members, where we were going to spend our Honeymoon!

After the spiritually Christ-honouring Wedding Service, photographs, lovely Wedding Reception at a Private Hotel off the Great Western Road, and more photographs, we quietly made our way out of the back door to the taxi to take us to the Central Station. Before we got there, we realised that we were being followed, and a group of family and friends were ready to give a hearty send off! Boarding the train, and changing at Carlisle, we finally reached the station nearest to Keswick.

Later in the evening of that same day we were just finishing our Evening Meal in the Guest House in the Heads, and we happened to look out of the window. What did we see? A certain young man carrying boxes and parcels very carefully to his room in the top of the guesthouse next door. It was none other than our dear friend and Best Man, Peter! So, while he was on one of his trips upstairs my new Bride Ann and I wrote on his car window, 'JUST MARRIED' and put confetti all over his car. We then returned to our own guesthouse. Suddenly Peter came down, read the words and scratched his head, all puzzled. So then we came out and had a great laugh! After that, Ann's family were informed as to where we were, and Ann and I had a wonderful Honeymoon in Lakeland scenery.

To God be the glory!

Footnote:
A word of explanation regarding the HALL FAMILY.

Sadly, only my dear brother Cyril was able to attend the Wedding, which he greatly enjoyed, and he represented the Hall family. At that time my mother was recovering from an operation, and my father felt he should look after Mum. Ann's parents and my parents had met over a meal at our home at Nazeing sometime previously. My sister Iris was pregnant and didn't have long to go, so she and her husband Patrick didn't relish the 400-mile journey to Glasgow. Finally, my elder sister Rosemarie and her husband Roger were in Australia.

They all sent gifts and their love.

10   The London City Mission

Valedictory Service

At the end of my studies at B.T.I. the Lord directed me to the London City Mission (L.C.M.), and thus early in January 1961 I commenced training with them. My home Church, Hoddesdon Baptist Church held a Valedictory Service for me on Sunday 29th January, setting me apart and sending me forth to preach the glorious Gospel of Christ. They presented me with a copy of Strong's *Exhaustive Concordance of the Bible*" commemorating that event, and which was signed by our Minister L.W. Jupp, with the words

> *2 Corinthians 2:14* "Now thanks be unto God, which always causeth us to triumph in Christ, and maketh manifest the savour of His knowledge in every place."

It was a most moving, Spiritual Service, at which Pastor Jupp gave a most appropriate message; but what stands out in my memory was the heart-felt challenge to me from our Deacon Mr. Bassett, to take the 'Flaming Torch of the Gospel of Christ' to men and women who need to be Saved – wherever He may lead – which I have been privileged to do for the past fifty-seven years. I can only give a brief report of that three-year period in my life, that is, my time with the L.C.M. from January 1961 to June 1964.

My four months **probationary training** was initially with Mr. Jack Bye, the Missionary based at Winscombe Street Mission at Highgate New Town, and later with Mr. Colin Walker who was Missionary to the Theatre Staff, working in the old Covenant Garden district and based at the Shorts Garden Medical Mission. (Fortunately, no medical treatment was in operation while I was there!) I had earlier failed the basic training, but the L.C.M. Committee, as it was called in those days, recommended in their wisdom that I have a second period with Mr. Colin Walker. Incidentally this situation was not the fault of Jack Bye or of the Rev. R. B. Otway, who taught the weekly Lecture Class with distinction: he sadly died well before his prime.

Mr. F. W. Wrintmore, Secretary for L.C.M. North of the Thames, who was literally my boss, and author of *"The Future of London'*, wrote me a personal letter: in it he said, *"Our* disappointments are *His* appointments", and I came to realise that this is true (see *Romans 8:28*). As you will shortly see, the Lord had some encouragements in store for me.

It was meanwhile difficult doing visitation Evangelism in the Russell Square and Regent Square areas of the city. It was good going with Colin Walker to the Royal Opera House during the day, and being able to go 'behind the scenes' (Russian Bolshoi Ballet Company) – the Opera House faces the Bow Street Police Station. Mr. Walker, a Yorkshire man, related well to people, and he had a commanding, but gracious way with him. During this period, I stayed in a flat above the then Headquarters of the L.C.M. in Eccleston Street, near to Victoria Coach Station, with Mr. and Mrs. Payne(?), who were fellow-missionaries.

Monthly H.Q. Service
Each month on pay day one hundred or so Missionaries gathered for a Service in the Bridewell Hall downstairs at H.Q. (the Headquarters of the L.C.M. has since moved to Tower Hill). It was wonderful to see all these godly men assembled together, and we usually had a well-known visiting preacher. Dr. John MacBeath, brother of Andrew (see Chapter 8), ministered the Word on one occasion, and gave us each a copy of one of his books. After completing the second probationary period satisfactorily I was moved to the Finsbury Park district to work half of the week on District evangelism, and the other half at FELLOWSHIP HOUSE, Welwyn Garden City, in Hertfordshire. This placement lasted for about eighteen months. The Lord provided accommodation at Haringey with Mr. Harold and Mrs. Hilda Pearce, with their children Graham and Christine. Harold was both Sunday School Superintendent and Boys Brigade Leader at Tollington Park Baptist Church, and was ably supported by Hilda – a fine couple.

It was about this time that Ann came down to London to live in a hostel at Hornsea Rise to get acclimatised to the City before our marriage. It took a lot of courage for her to leave her home, family, and settled work and church-life to find suitable employment in London, which she did on the occasion of her second visit. The Lord even gave her an office manager who was Scottish and, even better, from Glasgow, praise God! We continued our courtship, and were very happy at Tollington Park Baptist Church, where the minister was Rev. John Potter. T.P., as it was affectionately known, was a lovely Fellowship of God's people. After we were married, Harold and Hilda let Ann and I stay on in my old 'bed-sit' with boxes of wedding presents under the bed and everywhere. Later L.C.M. provided us with an upstairs flat at Hugon Road, Fulham, because we were then based at St. John's Church in the poorer Worlds End area of Chelsea, with the faithfully serving evangelical Vicar Rev. Geoffrey Barber.

Carolyn Appears at An Early Hour.

It was to be a memorable period for another reason, too.

Carolyn our eldest daughter was born at 3.00 a.m. on 11th September 1962 at Parsons Green Nursing Home. After visiting Mother and baby I walked home through the streets of Fulham at about 3.30 a.m. thankful for God's gift of a beautiful baby girl, and that Ann my wife and baby were well – and that I had become a father!

We worshipped when we could at Dawes Road Baptist Church, and we also faithfully attended services at St. Johns. We took Carolyn along in a carrycot, having to ride on two buses to get there. I did consistent visitation in the streets around the Church and in the Lots Road area, took the Sunday Covenanter Class, and faithfully read the Lessons Morning and Evening each Sunday: "Here beginneth the first verse of the Fourth Chapter of the Gospel of St. Luke." "Here endeth the Second Lesson". I didn't have the qualification to preach in the Church of England and that was at times frustrating to a person called to preach 'the unsearchable riches of Christ'. So, I would read over and pray over the passage of Scripture to be read, and pray that the Holy Spirit would speak through the words I read, and He did.

Whilst at St. Johns I did organise an OPEN-AIR SERVICE, with different people giving testimony to Christ's Saving Grace, and so the Word of God and Gospel were proclaimed across the road at the Worlds End. The CHELSEA TIMES had to describe the open-air service in their highbrow way as an 'Alfresco Service' but did give good coverage of it with a good accompanying picture.

In a street to the west of the Church, a dear Christian man who, sadly, was disabled had a Watch and Clock repair business. He and his wife were members of the Congregational Church in Edith Grove. Near the end of our time, I helped him get to the St. Stephen's Hospital to visit his wife who was receiving treatment there. Later, after God led me to take up an appointment as Scottish Secretary of The Railway Mission, he wrote me a moving letter to tell of his wife's death, and to express sincere thanks for all the help I had given him while at Chelsea.

One final comment: The Vicar gave us quite a surprise one Sunday by announcing the banns of his own wedding to a certain lady by the name of 'Anne', who was totally unknown to the Congregation, and who had been a Missionary with the Bible Churchmen's Missionary Society. Life is full of surprises.

On the sad side, there was even the murder of a young man just a short distance from St. John's Church, and the Metropolitan Police set up a Mobile Unit nearby to gather evidence. And on a positive side I did attend one game at Stamford Bridge, home of Chelsea Football Club, but I can't remember whom they played – or the result.

I got to know a blind man quite well, who lived in a flat just off the Kings Road: he impressed me in the way that he walked along the busy Kings Road with its heavy traffic; and he even Hoovered his flat himself.

11   The First Time I Flew in An Aeroplane

As a boy I used to see the different biplanes at Broxbourne Aerodrome, actually situated at the northern end of my home village of Nazeing, on the Hertfordshire-Essex border. In those days you could take a flight for as little as 10/- (50p). I dreamed of doing so, but never did go up. However, it was exciting to watch the planes take off and land. It was from this aerodrome that a plane took off and the pilot sensationally flew the aircraft under London's famous Tower Bridge in the in the fifties. I recall that the London Evening Standard had a picture of it on its front page that very evening. But it was from another airfield – Panshanger, on the outskirts of Welwyn Garden City – that I first entered air space.

It came about like this: whilst serving with the London City Mission I was for a while seconded for half of the week to Fellowship House, a Christian Church Centre run by the Carnegie family, in Welwyn Garden City. It was a unique situation – the cream of evangelical preachers occupied the pulpit it in this unique octagonal building in Tewin Road on the edge of the Industrial part of the second Garden City. Here came many famous preachers like Dr. Paul Rees of Minneapolis, Minnesota, and Dr. H. D. MacDonald, Vice-Principal of London Bible College to name but two.

My job was to do visitation evangelism, to lead and speak at the Ladies' Fellowship, and to engage in pastoral care ministry. I had been asked by Mr. F.H. Wrintmore, Secretary North of the Thames for the L.C.M., to undertake this important ministry, taking the place of a fellow-worker from South Wales who came from a socially deprived area and could not settle in an affluent environment. The eighteen months spent at Fellowship House was a spiritually fruitful period in the providence of God, about which I will tell more in the next Chapter, "*First Fruits for God's Glory*".

Which brings me to recount my first flight experience, which happened like this.

I was staying at the time with a fine Christian family by the name of Harold and Hilda Pearce, with Graham and Christine, at Harringay in North London, and from there travelled by train one Friday morning to Welwyn Garden City. On arrival, Mr. Donald Carnegie approached me and said – quite out of the blue – "Would you like to go Oxford with me by plane?" – that very morning. I was a bit taken aback: "Shouldn't I be working?" I said. He replied, "No, it will be alright since you have been working conscientiously," or words to that effect. He went on to say, "I am going to Panshanger Airfield to fly to Oxford to pick up my son Peter and bring him back." I was totally amazed, and didn't have time to get my passport! Not needed!

It is exciting when you step out in faith to follow the Lord, and don't know what surprises He has in store. So, we left in Mr. Carnegie's posh car, and in a few minutes, we arrived at Panshanger Airfield. He went straight to the hanger and led out a Cessna type plane. It was a clear summer's day and visibility was good, but I was a little apprehensive as we got seated etc. I said, "Mr. Carnegie, do you mind if we pray before take-off?" He was very understanding, and immediately prayed for the Lord's help on the journey. Contact was then made with the Control Tower, and before long we were up in the air with the plane's compass set for Oxford. (Incidentally, *Cambridge* had always had my support for the University Boat Race, having come from the north east side of London and living not far from the railway line to Cambridge.)

After about twenty minutes of enjoying magnificent views of the countryside on our smooth and exhilarating flight we arrived near Oxford, and ahead and below us were its famous Churches and University Spires. We had a perfect landing, and then walked over to the Airport Club House where we met up with Peter, who was studying art in Oxford. We enjoyed a welcome cup of coffee and a brief respite, and then we boarded the plane *en route* back to Panshanger. Donald had another surprise up his sleeve, unknown to me. As soon as we were airborne, he said to me, "Would you like see over your house and village of Nazeing?" I was again taken aback.

At Brookman's Park he set the compass for Southend-on-Sea, and it was not long before we had reached St Leonards Road, Nazeing. We circled over the road, and over my parents' house, but there was no one to be seen. This was before the days of Mobile Phones, so although my parents were on the phone I had no opportunity to let them know we were flying above them! As the plane circled, I got butterflies in the stomach, the only time this happened on the flight. It was a great privilege to see the village and my parents' home from the air, and I shall always be eternally grateful to Donald Carnegie for his kindness. On reflection, he may have just wanted company on the first part of the journey, but it was still a great privilege!

Many years later Ann and I renewed contact with Donald and his wife Marjorie in Jersey, Channel Islands, following an unexpected contact with their son Dr. David Carnegie. We were on holiday following the death of my parents; and then we met them again on subsequent Deputation visits for The Mission to Mobile Homes. Mr. Donald Carnegie also used the same plane to fly a team of Lecturers and Preachers from London Bible College to minister the Word of God and Christ's Gospel to the Independent Evangelical Churches in Greece.

12   First Fruits for God's Glory

We all rejoice in the natural birth of a boy or girl – each such event is a miracle. It is equally so with regard to spiritual re-birth, what Jesus called being 'born again' (*John 3*) or 'born from above' (*1 John*). We can never be sure when it will take place, as with human birth. In Christian ministry it is possible to faithfully preach the eternal 'Word of the Gospel' for a long time and see no obvious results. But God in His Sovereign mercy, as the Apostle says, works everything after "the counsel of His own will" (*Ephesians 1:11*).

On the other hand, it is also true that one can be faithfully serving the Lord and see souls saved in a short period of time, as I was privileged to see at Welwyn Garden City in 1961. We also have to remember what Paul also wrote to the Corinthian Church:

1 Corinthians 3:6 "I have planted, Apollos watered; but GOD gave the increase."

God alone by His Holy Spirit can make the seed germinate in people's hearts, the glory is His alone. Thus, it was in the providence of God that He should let me see two souls wonderfully saved, to his honour and glory.

A Converted Railwayman
Mr. A., a retired British Rail ticket collector, was at home suffering from cancer. I didn't know how it came about that regular visits were made to his house, but they did come about, and his wife approved of them and appreciated them. I started reading from *St. Luke's Gospel* in the chapters leading up to Christ's Cross and resurrection, and always had prayer with him, that the Lord would speak to him. It gave me the opportunity to present Christ Jesus who died in the place of sinners as our substitute, to pay for our sin. He suffered the punishment for our sin and I stressed the need to repent and have faith in Christ for forgiveness and Salvation.

As I read the Scriptures and prayed with our dear friend, he became aware that he was a sinner, as are we all in the eyes of a Holy God, the Holy Spirit bringing conviction of sin. After about the fourth or fifth visit he said with burning conviction "I've asked the Lord to forgive me all my sins". He had put his trust in Christ as his own personal Saviour. He had obviously realised he hadn't long in this life: how wonderful that he had made his peace with God while there was time, and that he was now rejoicing in the assurance of Christ as his own Saviour and Lord. It was not very long afterwards that the Lord called him home.

His dear wife asked that I attend the Crematorium service, where I had a good opportunity to witness to the family individually. I look forward to meeting our dear friend in Heaven.

Converted in Her Own Kitchen
Mrs. Mardell, a married lady in her late twenties, came regularly to the Ladies' Meeting at Fellowship House, Welwyn Garden City. She had heard the truths of the Gospel over a number of months and was genuinely interested. She came with her boy of about four years of age, who was very well behaved.

I visited her one day in her kitchen and read *1 John 5:11-13*, then prayed and spoke to her firstly about the Lord Jesus from *Romans 5:8*: "But God commendeth His love toward us, in that, while we were yet sinners, Christ died for us". Endeavouring to present and explain what the Christ accomplished on the Cross of Calvary, in dying in the place of sinners and shedding His precious blood to redeem sinners and bring about reconciliation and forgiveness, I then read:

> *1 John 5:11-12* "And this is the record, that God hath given to us eternal life, and this life is in His Son. He that hath the Son hath life; and he that hath not the Son of God hath not life."

God gives us eternal life in the Lord Jesus. If you receive Jesus into your heart and life, you have Eternal Life. I then underlined the amazing statement of the next verse:

> *1 John 5:13* "These things have I written unto you that believe on the name of the Son of God; that you may KNOW that you have Eternal Life".

I stressed that you can not only be *Saved* by God's grace but can also have the *assurance* that you are saved! I told her, "If you repent of your sins, put your trust in Christ Who died for your sins and receive Him as your personal Saviour you can know and have the definite assurance that you have Eternal Life." Then before leaving I prayed a simple prayer of repentance for sin, thanked God that Jesus had died for her sins and encouraged her to receive Christ into her heart and life and know forgiveness and Salvation.

A week or ten days later I met Mrs. Mardell again. She thanked me for the recent visit to her home, told me that she had responded to the Gospel of Christ that very day in her own kitchen, and said, "I felt a sense of great joy: I felt cleaner inside".

True, authentic notes of the Gospel are:

A) The Joy Of Salvation
> *Luke 2:10* "Behold I bring you good tidings of great joy, which shall be to all people."

As the old chorus expresses it:

> *If you want joy, real joy, wonderful joy*
> *Let Jesus come into your heart.*
> *Your sins, He'll take away*
> *Your night He'll turn to day.*

Or, as *Luke 15:10* tells us: "There is joy in the presence of the angels of God over one sinner that repenteth."

B) **A Clean Heart**

"I felt cleaner inside…"

> *1 John 1:7* "The blood of Jesus Christ His Son cleanseth us from all sin."

What peace of heart follows being washed in Jesus' blood – it passes all understanding!

This dear lady later emigrated with her husband and family to Australia, and contact was lost. No doubt one day we will meet her in heaven, when perhaps we will learn more of her life and of how God blessed and used her.

13 My Time in Scotland with the Railway Mission

First: how did I come to be *with* the Railway Mission?

As I have already mentioned, I felt frustrated because I didn't have the opportunity to preach Christ regularly each Lord's Day with my position in the London City Mission. Thus, I prayed much for an opening of the Lord's choice. Having noticed an advertisement for a Scottish Secretary for the Railway Mission, I applied, and met Mr. Hodgson of the Scottish Committee who was visiting London.

Then on Friday 22nd May 1964 I went by the Royal Scott train to Glasgow, and there was met by Miss Eva Kilner. Providentially, at the same time a flat was advertised in Beith, Ayrshire, and Miss Kilner took me to see it. On the Saturday afternoon, I was interviewed by the Scottish Committee in Glasgow and was offered the job, and that evening I flew back to London with BEA. Praise God! My meditation had been: *Psalm 23* "He leadeth me ... I will fear no evil: for Thou art with me".

The Railway Mission, which commenced in 1881 – no doubt influenced by the 1859 Revival – became a great soul-winning agency among the 400,000 railwaymen, but a century later the scene had changed considerably. In 1964 when I joined it as Secretary of the Scottish Section it was, in Scotland at least, in terminal decline. There were, thank God, some exceptions – needing some explanations. What do I mean? Some Railway Missions had become Evangelical Churches, for example in Brighton, Swindon, Carlisle, and Maryhill (Glasgow), to name a few – there were others, too. They were then constituted as Independent Evangelical Churches, which in that way was good, as evangelism had come full course. Some linked up with the F.I.E.C. and had their own full or part-time pastors.

Now to go back to the situation in Scotland at that time: many Railway Mission Halls North of the Border had by then (1964) no working railwaymen, and only a few retired railwaymen, attending.

By way of further explanation, Maryhill Evangelical Church, formerly a Railway Mission Hall, was then a good evangelical Church, with a modern building. Although without a pastor as such, they had excellent godly men who were good elders: Mr. David Currie and Mr. Sam McIlroy. They were also conductors of the fine mixed Choir. They took part, with others, as conductors for the famous Male Voice Choir Festivals, founded by Mr. James McRoberts, held at the Tabernacle Church in Glasgow. One of my sweetest joys was to hear them singing the well-known CHRISTMAS CAROLS at the old St. Enoch's station concourse, and winsomely present the Lord Jesus Christ, who came into the world to SAVE sinners. With passengers on the way home from work, some stopped and listened to the heavenly message, while others quickly went on their way reminded of the amazing grace of God.

Changes at Edinburgh Gorgie

Edinburgh at that time had only one Railway Mission Hall – at Gorgie, near to the Heart of Midlothian Football Ground. Mr. Robert Johnson, a very capable Clerk of the Scottish High Court, was its leader. I went over to Edinburgh shortly after I was appointed and preached in the Scottish Capital on God's message to the Apostle Paul at Corinth:

> *Acts 18:10* "For I am with thee, and no man shall set on thee to hurt thee: for I have much people in this City."

That I felt was an appropriate message – with its message of the Cross of Christ. Mr. Robert Johnson was cordial, but didn't fully reveal his hand at that point. Then, in my second year, he instructed his lawyer in Edinburgh to telephone me at the Railway Mission office in the Christian Institute in Glasgow to tell me that the Edinburgh branch of the Railway Mission had decided to become independent, as the 'Gorgie Gospel Mission', and that he was also to resign as a member of the Scottish Committee.

I respected his decision and that of the friends at Gorgie, but only wished that he had spoken to me personally, rather than through his lawyer. It weakened my hand, and that of the Scottish Committee, to further the work of the Railway Mission in Scotland. Many years later his daughter graciously arranged for me to tell of the work of The Mission to Mobile Homes at the said Gorgie Gospel Mission, which I much

34

appreciated, and there enjoyed good fellowship. Interestingly, it was situated next to, or almost next to, the famous Heart of Midlothian Football Ground.

Some Observations

The people in the Railway Mission Halls were lovely Evangelical Christian men and women, who loved the Word of God and our LORD JESUS CHRIST. I am in touch with some of them even to the present day (2019), but many others have since been called home to Heaven. It is difficult to mention names, as I am bound to leave some worthy names out. However, a few names, like those of our brothers Duncan Black and Derek Anderson, will appear later as I tell of Mission to Mobile Homes outreach and supporting ministry.

Brief Reports of Railway Evangelism

Mr. W. Fergusson of Meadow Side, Beith, a surface-man* was checking the Largs Line just outside Kilwinning Station when a roof was blown off a hut and knocked him down on to the line, breaking both his legs and pinning them to the line. If the men in the hut hadn't come to his help immediately and rescued him he might have lost his life. This incident happened just after 12 noon.

I visited him in Kilmarnock Hospital. He realised that his life had been spared and when I explained the Way of Salvation through Christ's shed blood – "That's right" he said "both my parents were Christians – my father was a preacher. My brother attends Bethany Hall in Beith." At this moment he paused: I took it to mean that he suddenly realised that he was not following in their footsteps. May this prove to have been a turning point in his life. I think at this point I must have prayed with him and left the Hospital, but Ann visited his wife and daughter at their home and had prayer with them.

Report in the 'Railway Signal'** – Scottish Edition.
'A LIFT-UP!'

At Glengarnock Station, on the Ayr Line on Friday 16th December 1966 a ganger and his team of workers were busy lifting the line which had gradually, through the weight of the Rolling Stock, become sunken below the required level. Chips were cleared in-between the rails and a jack used to raise the line.

Mr. Hector Hall, rail-evangelist, was waiting for a train and told the men that Christ came to raise them from pit of sin, and give them new life and a new song to sing; if they will repent and trust Him. They each received 'A Railway Signal'. Please pray for such men to be saved.

The next chapter will tell of some of the things that God accomplished during my three years with the Scottish Section of the Railway Mission.

* A railway surface-man, known in England as a platelayer, was responsible for the upkeep and safety of the track.

** The *"Railway Signal"* was the magazine leaflet published and issued by the Railway Mission.

14   Railway Mission Scottish Secretary 1964-67
What was accomplished during those three years
*Only eternity will **fully** reveal what God accomplished.*

(Actually, I am English, and a kilt is bit too cold for me in the Scottish Winters…) From the beginning, God provided a nice flat for Ann, the family and myself in Beith, Ayrshire. As I started work as Secretary, Dundee Railway Mission was re-opened under the leadership of my good friend Mr. Sinclair Abbot. This was the report in the Scottish ***Railway Signal***:

DUNDEE BRANCH RE-OPENS
Mr. Sinclair Abbot, Superintendent of the above Branch, informs me that their Sunday School re-commences on Sunday 10th October at 2.30 pm.

As well as Mr. Abbot, there are two other young men who will assist as teachers namely Robert Middleton and Henry Laing (both brought up in the Railway Mission), making an all-male trio of teachers!

During the Summer, they worked hard redecorating the large South room in time for this session. What is more, they have got hand-bills printed and plan to go out and bring the children in.

We pray that they may be greatly used of God in reaching boys and girls with the saving knowledge of Jesus Christ.

"WE ARE LABOURERS TOGETHER WITH GOD"

1 Corinthians 3:9

The Scottish Office & Railway Evangelism
During my time with the Railway Mission in Scotland I often witnessed to railway staff at Glasgow Central Station, and to local station

staff as I travelled *en route* to meetings and to the R.M. Office in the Christian Institute, in Bothwell Street, Glasgow. I had no staff, but was ably supported by members of the Scottish Committee, and a dear lady from the Glasgow Foundry Boys Society* made sure that I had a cup of tea mid-morning and mid-afternoon. (*This was then a mission to provide education and training for young lads working in the local Iron foundries.)

One of my privileges as Scottish Secretary, was a to be given a First Class Pass on the railway network from Aberdeen and Inverness and all stations south to Carlisle! The FIRST NORTH EAST AREA RALLY was held on Saturday 10th September 1966 in DUNDEE RAILWAY MISSION in Taylors Lane, and this was a time of encouragement and blessing. Friends came from different parts of Scotland, as well as from the local Montrose Branch. Mr. Sinclair Abbot warmly welcomed us on behalf of the Mission fellowship. As Scottish Secretary of the Railway Mission, I gave a brief Report of the Lord's leading and guiding.

Then after prayer and a hymn I introduced our Guest Speaker Pastor Andrew Kennedy of Dawes Road Baptist Church, Fulham, London. He had been a missionary with Overseas Missionary Fellowship (O.M.F.). (When we were with the London City Mission we had worshiped whenever possible at Dawes Road Baptist Church.) He read from *Isaiah Chapter 40* and gave a wonderful exposition of the Greatness of God – the Everlasting GOD whose power sustains, controls, and rules the whole universe that He created. It is not always that one can remember a message given over 50 years ago! The ladies prepared a tea for us, and we all enjoyed fellowship together before returning home, and thinking what a great God we have.

Salmon Leaping & Summer Camp 22nd – 29th July 1967
I went by train to Pitlochry, and while waiting there for the Coach Party from Dundee Railway Mission I crossed the river bridge and had the unexpected pleasure and privilege to see one of the wonders of God's Creation – Salmon leaping up out of the water with obvious delight. What a sight it was – I couldn't stop watching: what joy God gave me that day. Strangely, there was no one else about to share it with.

The friends from Dundee eventually arrived and warm greetings exchanged and we travelled on to the Camp Site. It was wet and damp over the first weekend, and the floor of the meeting tent was spongy under foot, but on the Lord's Day the presence of God was experienced in the meetings and young people were attentive to hear Gods Word and Gospel. But when Monday morning came the sun came out, and the weather turned glorious for the rest of the week. Rannoch Moor, where our camp was situated, is an extremely beautiful area of Perthshire. On one trip, we walked about five miles before climbing a small mountain, and then had to walk five miles back on the return. Our ankles ached but the fellowship was great. The Dundee Team carried out their Bible Teaching Programme with the children with great enthusiasm during the week of the Camp. We thank Sinclair and his helpers for arranging such a lovely camp: the food was good, and we praised God for good weather.

(I had actually completed my time with the Railway Mission that summer, but was asked to return to be chaplain for this Summer Camp. It was a pleasure and a privilege!)

Worthy Men of Bathgate

The Railway ceased to have a station in Bathgate, but the Mission there continued under the name of Bethany Hall (Mr. and Mrs. James Purves), and there I often preached the Word and Gospel. James was the brother of Jock Purves, World Evangelization Crusade (WEC) missionary and author of *'Fair Sunshine – a history of the Scottish Covenanters'*.

Bethany Hall later became, with a new building, Sir James Simpson Memorial Hall, named after the famous Bathgate doctor, Sir James Young Simpson. His father had a baker's shop in the town. He studied at Edinburgh University, where he later became professor of Midwifery. He used Chloroform as an anaesthetic, and was the first, in 1847, to use it in childbirth cases. He was once asked what was his greatest discovery? He thought for a moment, and then answered, "That I am a great sinner and Jesus Christ is a GREAT SAVIOUR". He was created a baronet in 1866, thus becoming Sir James Simpson, no doubt in recognition of his worthy contributions to medical science.

First South West Area Rally
At the Bonnyton Mission, Kilmarnock, Ayrshire
(Saturday 22nd April 1967)

It was a good spiritual Rally and we were warmly welcomed by Miss Noble and Mr. & Mrs. McCrone, and their team of helpers. It was an encouragement to them. Mr. George Scott, Chairman of Scottish Railway Mission, brought greetings from the Glasgow Branches. The Rally ended with good fellowship over Tea, prepared by the ladies.

Report of Gospel Outreach at Kilmarnock Station

After a lot of prayer, prior to the Area Rally, I visited the Railway Staff at the Kilmarnock Station Booking Office, Parcel Office, Freight Depot, Telegraph & Enquiry Office – and the al-important Signal Box. I also met fitters, porters, drivers and vehicle drivers. Thus, probably fifty or so men were witnessed to and given the *Evangelist* and *Railway Signals* leaflets, and invitations to the Rally. One young man said, "There must be something in this." Cliff Richard has come to personal faith through reading the Bible. Another said that he was an atheist and asked me, "What do you think of Billy Graham?" I told a fitter to "Get plugged-in to the power of God through faith in Christ." A man in the Signal Box knew our brother Oswald Campbell, who attends Bonnyton Mission Hall.

Although it was disappointing that no new faces from the Rail-Network at Kilmarnock Station attended the Area Rally, ***nevertheless*** it showed that there were still men who had the courage to go to them at their work place and boldly and unashamedly witness to the POWER OF CHRIST TO SAVE SINNERS and TRANSFORM LIVES.

Barassie Rail-Works Meeting

Each month on a Thursday I went by train to Troon to chair the Barassie Rail-Works Lunch Time Meeting, which was held in the Canteen. There we had some fifty to sixty men listen to the Gospel, with local ministers and laymen speaking. On one occasion Mr. Abbott from Scottish Aviation, Prestwick, brought a model aircraft along and proclaimed Christ as Creator and Saviour, to rapt attention. We had just a ten-minute "slot", but God's Word and Christ's Saving grace were proclaimed. Good contacts were made, and good conversations had with the men.

Future Ministry

About the turn of the year 1966-67 the Scottish Committee, with whom I had always had cordial relations, informed me that as funds were getting low (I had only a very modest salary), then should an opening come for Christian ministry elsewhere, I should take it. I wasn't looking for a change, and truly they didn't want to have to terminate my employment.

God's Apprenticeship

My three-and-a-half years with the London City Mission trained me well as a personal Evangelist. My almost three years with the Railway Mission, Scottish Section, enabled me to develop preaching and organizational skills i.e. arranging Meetings, Area Rallies and Conferences. Furthermore, it became my responsibility to edit the Scottish *Railway Signal*, in which our brother Alan Graham, the former editor, gave me every assistance. Since my father was an Accountant, that meant I always had good "money sense", and had never bothered about my pocket money – but I did pester my father about a bicycle!

Mr. Ewert Helyar, General Secretary of the Railway Mission in England for many years, gave good leadership of the Mission, and good Biblical ministry. I understand from friends that he is still alive at the time of writing (2017), aged 95 years.

Footnote:
On 13th April, 1966, my dear wife Ann gave birth to our beloved second daughter **Sharon Moira Hall** in Irvine Central Hospital. Truly God's gift, and a sister for Carolyn. Ann's mum, Mrs. Helen Creighton, came and stayed with us, and was a great help!

The next Chapter begins to reveal God's outworking of His Plan for our lives and the area of our future ministry.

15   The Call of God to Mobile Home Park People

"Faith is taking God at His Word" *Samuel Rutherford*

In the spring of 1967 I was working in Scotland with Scottish Section of The Railway Mission as Scottish Secretary, although I am English myself! It was a changing situation, and many of their mission halls no longer had railwaymen attending. Some were in decline, whilst a few had come full circle and were now established Evangelical Churches. The Scottish Committee, with whom I had an excellent relationship, did not give me the sack, but they did tell me to take any opportunity that might come my way in the way of employment. As I waited on the Lord and travelled extensively across Scotland – and occasionally in England – the Lord drew my attention to people residing on residential Caravan Parks i.e. "Caravan dwellers".

On the evening of 5th April – after much prayer – I visited the West Ferry Mobile Home Park near Langbank on the Clyde estuary to find out more. The owner's son having given me permission, I went from one caravan to another and found many spiritually needy people unreached with the Gospel of Christ, and without any real church connection. In those homes where people did invite me in I shared my testimony of the

Lord's Saving grace. It was dark as I left the park and the lights of the park and the mobile homes reflected in the River Clyde, giving its own beauty. My heart was excited as I walked back to the station *en route* home to Ann and family. *Did God want me to work amongst such people?* My diary for that date reads, "Wonderfully guided of God". However, the Lord must confirm through His Word.

At this time, I did visit the then Stirling Library in Glasgow to do a little research on mobile home parks. These were very well established in North America, but there was not a lot of information on the British scene. Also, at this time there came into my hands a copy of the Southern Baptist (USA) magazine, which carried a mobile home story.

However, the Lord's confirmation came on 6th May 1967. Ever since my conversion in June 1953 my custom has been to read a chapter from the Old Testament in the morning, and a similar portion from the New Testament in the evening consecutively, so as to get the whole counsel of God. That morning the reading was from *Numbers Chapter 13* – the "Spy Chapter". *Verse 2* says *"The LORD spake unto Moses, saying, Send thou men, that they may SEARCH the land of CANAAN, which I GIVE unto the Children of Israel: of every tribe... shall ye send a man, every one a ruler among them."* The twelve spies were given specific instructions concerning type of people, the security of the cities (or lack thereof) and the fruitfulness of the land. They completed their task after forty days and returned to Moses at Kadesh with their report. Actually, there were two reports.

1. The Evil Report, which saw all the difficulties. The cities walled high, the people strong as giants and "we were like grasshoppers" in comparison. Their position was summed up in four words in *verse 31* "WE BE NOT ABLE" i.e. to conquer the land. This was the verdict of the MAJORITY. Needless to say, the majority is not always right, as the children's chorus sums it up:

> *Twelve men went to spy out Canaan,*
> *Ten were bad and two were good,*
> *What were they there to spy in Canaan*
> *Ten were bad and two were good*
>
> *Some saw giants great and small,*
> *Some saw grapes in clusters full,*
> *Some saw that God was in it all,*
> *Ten were bad and two were good.*

41

2 The Good Report was given by Caleb and supported by just one other significant person, Joshua. Indeed, a MINORITY report by two out of the twelve. God used the whole Spy Story to speak to me, but in particular *verse 30*:

> *Numbers 13:30* "And Caleb stilled the people before Moses, and said, Let us GO UP AT ONCE, and possess it (the Promised Land); for WE ARE WELL ABLE to overcome it."
> *(With the Lord's help – of course.)*

The Lord said to me, don't be fearful like the faithless spies but be like Caleb and Joshua and GO FORWARD in FAITH and possess the Mobile Home Parks across Scotland for God. "WE ARE WELL ABLE" – yes, you may be married with a wife and two young children to support, but I will provide!

> *Faith, mighty faith, the promise sees,*
> *And looks to God alone,*
> *Laughs at impossibilities,*
> *And cries – it shall be done!*
>
> *(Charles Wesley)*

The Radio announced just prior to the 9 am news that morning that "British Forces returning to the U.K. from Aden would be housed in MOBILE HOMES." It also happened the same day that the Scottish Committee of the Railway Mission would be meeting in the afternoon in Glasgow. As confirmation had been clearly given by God, I felt it was the right time to give in my resignation to take effect at the end of the month, after three and a half memorable years with the Railway Mission in Scotland.

Another significant verse that the Lord spoke to me was:

> *Numbers 14:8*: "If the LORD DELIGHT in US, THEN HE WILL BRING US INTO THIS LAND."

On Sunday 4th June 1967 I gave a brief report of mobile home evangelism at The Mains Mission (Ayrshire Christian Union) Hall, Beith. A day or two later Mrs. K. said that she and her daughter would give £1 per month toward our support – Praise God! – the first of many. On the following day, Monday 5th June, I went into the Railway Mission office in the Christian Institute next to the old Bible Training Institute in Bothwell Street, Glasgow, to hand over the reins to Alex Watt and Jim Robertson, who were to "hold the fort". On return home at Glengarnock Station (the last use of my special 1st Class Rail Pass!) Dr Arthur

Jamieson kindly gave a friend and I a lift to Beith in his car. It was the decisive day of the Six-Day Arab-Israeli War. On the way Dr Arthur mentioned that God had promised the whole of the Holy Land to Israel – see *Joshua 1:4*, just to quote one verse of many.

16   Outreach Across Central Scotland
from Ayr to Edinburgh – July to October 1967

Much prayer went up for the Lord's Divine guidance in this visitation.

Brief excerpts from the 2nd "Mission to Mobile Homes" Prayer Letter sent out from 34 Dairy Road, Beith, Ayrshire on 21st September 1967.

Psalm126:3 "The LORD hath done great things for us; whereof we are glad."

Dear Christian Friends,

"Many thanks for your prayers which the Lord has abundantly answered.

We praise the Lord that residential Caravan Parks have been visited in Scotland, from Wemyss Bay on the west to Edinburgh on the east, and many people in spiritual need have been encouraged to repent and believe the Gospel."

....

"Christian literature is left at each home, and it is rarely refused. At Wemyss Bay a Roman Catholic lady told me she had read right through the 'Emergency Post', which I had left on a previous visit. She and her sister invited me in and I was able to read from John's Gospel Chapter 14 and explain that Christ was the only way to Heaven. They both received a copy of this Gospel to read for themselves, as they didn't possess a Bible."

"At Bellshill, Lanarkshire, a man said 'You've got courage, coming round on your own'. I replied 'One with God, is a majority'"

A later chapter will tell an interesting story.
Proverbs 24:27 "Prepare thy work without, and make it fit for thyself in the field; and afterwards build thine house."

The Lord impressed this truth on my mind and heart. (Earlier I had travelled down to Colne in Lancashire to see a house to rent, but it was unsuitable.) We needed a more centrally situated house, and the Lord had the matter in hand. Doors had been tried in Scotland but to no avail. So we were looking for, and praying for, a home placed more centrally to the U.K. as a whole, about which more later in this chapter.

Erskine Ferry Caravan Park

This small residential Caravan Park was situated just up from the river Clyde, with a lovely view of the river. People sadly had to move off the site when they commenced working on the magnificent 'Erskine Suspension Bridge'. (I think Duncan Black and I visited the Park just when this was happening.)

Now back to 1967! My memory recalls a teacher in training at Jordanhill College who had real doubts with regard to the authority and reliability of the Bible. She was of the Church of Scotland background. Firstly, I gave her my testimony of Christ's Saving Grace, and how the Bible came alive to me, after my conversion. The Bible is totally reliable – it is the Word of the Living God. Inspired by God the Holy Spirit, I trust I was a help to her. Also, on this Park I met a couple: the wife was probably Scottish and the husband said he came from Lincolnshire, England. In those days Lincolnshire was totally unknown to me.

What was more interesting was that he was a heavyweight boxer – not surprising, as he was a well-built man. He and his wife invited me in to their mobile home and no punches were pulled(!) in declaring the Gospel of Christ, who saves repenting sinners. All, no doubt, over a welcome cup of tea… The last time they were visited they were expecting to get a new house in the new Erskine Town, then yet to be built.

Uddingston Caravan Park

A few words about this Park, situated on higher ground.

I met Mr. Brown, the owner, on 1st August 1967 on a bus coming out of Renfrew Street Bus Station, Glasgow. He recognised me – he was at that time one of the Directors of the Bible Society of Scotland. He had given me permission at an earlier date to visit the residents: as we talked on the bus he gave me a promise of encouragement from:

> *2 Chronicles 15:7* "BE YE STRONG therefore, and LET NOT YOUR HANDS BE WEAK: FOR YOUR WORK SHALL BE REWARDED"

GOD later fulfilled this promise to us.

Then there was a lot of prayer and waiting on God regarding my next important assignment: The Mobile Home Parks at Loanhead. We will quote the second Prayer Letter again:

"We praise the Lord for His guiding hand. A few miles South of Edinburgh, near Loanhead, Midlothian, is a large Park of 200 Mobile Homes, with the Pentland Hills in the background (this park I had passed close by on the occasion of preaching at Peebles's Railway Mission).

The owner, Mr. Londi, in giving me permission to visit commented, 'You might do some good'. I came across two Christian Couples, Alastair and Carol MacKenzie (Pentecostal) and Alex and Catherine Brady (Open Christian Brethren). Alex sings with the 'Zion Quartet'. I also met a Christian lady Doctor, Valerie H. (Anglican) – an Anaesthetist at the Western Hospital, Edinburgh. I gave out tracts to a number of children who suddenly appeared – like a swarm of bees – but they told me they didn't attend a Sunday School. The nearest is a mile away. So I mentioned the need of a Sunday School on the Park to the above Christian friends, who said they had felt exercised about the spiritual need of the children, but nothing definite had been arranged. We then decided (after prayer) to commence a Sunday School when the children return to day School, in three available homes. Two meetings have been held to discuss plans and the School will commence on Sunday 1st October (D.V.).

Parents have shown a real interest, and the site owner approves. The team of teachers, led by Alex Brady, are keen to serve the Lord where He has placed them, and they are vising each family on the site (Nivensknowe Park) to ascertain details of all the children. We assure them of our prayers.

We praise the Lord for <u>His faithfulness</u> in supplying our every need, through His people. We thank all who have given so generously and sacrificially. We praise the Lord for providing a more centrally situated house to rent, as a base, with sufficient accommodation – 3 bedrooms etc. – for my family. Address: 1 PRINCE OF WALES ROW, MOULTON, Northants.

Prayer Fuel:
1. *800 people given Christian Literature. Pray for conviction of sin.*
2. *Pray for a Scot with a passion for souls. For follow-up.*
3. *Removal to Moulton on 7th October. Mobile Home Evangelism in the North of England.*
4. *Guidance in choice of the right people for Mission Council, and preparation of Magazine.*

With kind regards,
                    Cordially yours in Christ, HECTOR & ANN HALL"

Footnotes to this chapter:

A) Pioneer Days in Scotland

The early pioneer days were wonderful. People were open to the Gospel, and the Scots were most hospitable. Ann's family were wondering whether we were doing the right thing; as time went on they realised we were and keenly supported us. The Lord always vindicates His servants, who step out in faith in obedience to His call. We didn't have a motor-car at that point, but I still went out with the Gospel of Christ.

I used to prepare in the morning, have an early lunch, and then leave home using public transport. In some places there was no transport, I would pray and wait at a suitable junction and if necessary indicate a lift was needed. A car would stop and the driver would ask, "Where are you going to? Jump in." My Caravan Sites Handbook told me where the Caravan Park was situated i.e. off a certain A. or B. road. Next to my Bible, this Caravan Sites Handbook was the most useful tool at that time to get to the Parks. Many a good spiritual conversation was had with a kind driver *en route*. Ann would be praying at home for God to richly bless and guide.

Incidentally, I always dressed tidily with collar and tie etc., and carried a brief case. To be the best for Jesus.

B) Early Days Of The MMH – Unsolicited Letters.

20ᵗʰ Sept 1967. From Tom Smith. Irvine, Ayrshire.

"Dear Brother Hall,

Just a little sweet note in answer to your ever welcome and interesting letters for it is good to know that you are pushing the battle to the gate, for there is no work under the sun like witness for our ever-present Lord and Saviour Jesus Christ."

30ᵗʰ September 1967

                    Kilmarnock, Ayrshire

"Dear Hector,

Many thanks for your letter. I am so glad that the Lord is blessing your ministry to those who have no permanent homes such as we have…

It is heartening to read of your work amongst the boys and girls. We do long that they may be led to the Lord while tender in years."

Elizabeth Noble.

21ˢᵗ August 1967

Beith, Ayrshire.

"Dear Hector,

This is just a short note to say how much I respect and admire the work you are doing. Last Sunday I was shown that the money which was just lying idle could be put to good use in your hands. Please don't mention this letter or its contents to any of the others."

Yours in His service,
W.

----

17   God Found Us A House

Proverbs 24:27 "Prepare thy work without, and make it fit for thyself in the field; and afterwards build thine house."

The Lord impressed the truth of this verse on my mind and heart – that is, to get on with presenting personally the Gospel of CHRIST to people on the residential Caravan Parks, and He would deal with the practical needs. It was in late August or early September of 1967 when we were in Scotland but "waiting on God" for a suitable house to rent in central England. God had not opened the door to accommodation in Scotland, and on visiting a property in Colne, Lancashire, I found the house unsuitable. One day, however, I picked up a copy of 'The Christian' Newspaper and in it was an advertisement:

*'A 3 bedroom house to rent in Moulton, Northampton.
Rent £2.50 per week.'*

The paper by then was three weeks old – I said to Ann, "It will be gone by now". But after prayer – not being able to get the matter out of my mind – I felt I must write to the owner. A week later a letter arrived to say the house was still available, if we wanted it. It appeared that the owner had received many applications, but then a Salvation Army couple who were due to take the house turned it down at the last minute. It was then that our letter had arrived – God was obviously working in answer to our prayers. As William Cowper wrote *"GOD moves in a mysterious way His wonders to perform"*. We learnt later that the owner's mother's maiden name was Hall! It is strange how big decisions turn on little things sometimes.

Travel to see the House – and a Flexible Return

I had expended a lot of money going down to Colne, to no effect. So, a single rail ticket was bought to Northampton to enable me to meet the owner of the house in Moulton at the appointed time and date. The return arrangements were left flexible! My journey to Moulton went well and I met Cyril the owner who kindly showed me over the house: it seemed to be just what we needed, and the rent asked was very reasonable. However, where was I now to stay the night?

I didn't ask Cyril, and he didn't offer me a bed for the night but instead took me round to the 'Poplars Hotel' with Bed and Breakfast arranged for Seventeen & Sixpence. However, there was a little problem. As Cyril was present I didn't feel I could tell the proprietor of the Hotel that I would need to go in to Northampton the following morning to get money out of the building society. So, it was the next morning when I revealed this information to the Proprietor, and he was not very happy – I think he had had some problems with Scots from Corby. And he would have seen my Christian name 'Hector', a name popular in Scotland. (Nobody else thinks I am Scottish – I had better get a kilt!)

So, he said, "You will have to leave your case behind as security". The local bus was boarded and into Northampton I went; I withdrew money from the building society, then returned to Moulton village and the 'Poplars Hotel' where I duly paid my bill. This meant that my return to Scotland commenced a couple of hours later than intended. However, GOD knows about these things.

A Wait at Ferrybridge

I went *via* Kettering to Corby, and then the route must have been with different lifts to Newark and *via* the A1 to Doncaster. Thus I progressed, eventually arriving mid-afternoon at Ferrybridge with its Power Station and Cooling Towers. This will always stick in my memory, because for some unknown reason no car or vehicle would stop to give me a lift. By then of course half the journey had been completed. Fortunately, it was summer time, and the weather was good. It certainly concentrated prayer, and God knew all about it. "Thou God seest me," said Hagar (*Genesis*

16:13). The Lord indeed had it all in hand: some prayers are answered immediately, for others we have to wait for God's time.

Suddenly, a car stopped with two young men in it. They were, PRAISE GOD, going all the way to the Hamilton area, just south of Glasgow. From there I could easily get public transport to Glasgow and then out to Beith by bus. At home ANN was beginning to get anxious, as it was now about 8 pm in the evening. There were no mobile phones in those days, and there had not been any opportunity for me to phone her for most of the day. So she phoned her Dad, who kindly went out to Beith, to give any support or comfort that might be needed.

As it worked out he came out at about 9 pm and I arrived home shortly afterwards. We do Praise God for watching over us in answer to prayer, and in no way was I over-concerned, but I did understand Ann's natural concern. She was delighted not only in my safe arrival home, but with the good news of a three-bedroom house in a pleasant Northamptonshire Village. As also were Carolyn and Sharon. This end-terraced house was a few minutes from the local Library, shops, and Primary School. Also, nearby was a Baptist Church, famously connected with the pioneer missionary William Carey. Sadly, we were to find this church dwelt upon its famous past, and had little concern for the Salvation of lost souls in the village when we arrived in 1967.

The house also had some useful outbuildings. The Washroom was easily changed into a study that looked out on the garden. And the Coal Shed was later transformed into a Meeting Room – but that is another story for a later chapter!

18   Going South to Northampton

The removal of all our household goods and effects from Morrishill, Beith, Ayrshire, Scotland took place on Saturday morning 7th October 1967, for transporting to our new home in Moulton, Northampton. Our host Eva Kilner kindly gave us lunch – she was so good to us while we stayed at Morrishill. We must have gone to Ann's brothers and sisters flat in Glasgow and stayed with them overnight until Sunday night. Then, at 11:35pm, we got a taxi to Glasgow Central Station, to travel overnight ready for the removal people to arrive in Moulton at 10.15am on the Monday morning. Ann's family had also been so kind and helpful to us.

We had had a memorable three years in Ayrshire as I served as Scottish Secretary for the Railway Mission, and we had made many friends.

...But to retrace our steps a little: We arrived at Glasgow Central Station just as the train was about to leave for London Kings Cross. A Reservation attendant immediately recognised me, and quickly opened the door of a First Class compartment and removed the reservation notice from the window. We smiled as we got in, as I no longer had a 1st Class pass (that had gone when I left the Railway Mission!). *En route* we had to change trains at Carlisle, but no time to explain the details of the journey here...

Our Place of God's Appointment

The removal people at Lunn's couldn't understand the contrast between the beautiful flat we had occupied in a large house with grounds which we were leaving behind in Beith, to move to an end terrace house with not even tarmacadam on the road outside. However, we were happy – **it was the place of God's appointment**. Carolyn aged 7 years and Sharon aged 4½ years were excited.

The house in Moulton was unusual: it had been the Prince of Wales Public House fifty years earlier – needless to say, we were teetotal! The house had been modernised by the architect owner, but nonetheless the removal people had to remove the wooden stair banisters by unscrewing them to get the furniture to the upstairs bedrooms. Mrs. L the owner's mother – a kindly lady who lived with the owner's sister next door – warmly welcomed us and had warm soup ready for us, and we were able to show love to them in return.

Initially things were very difficult financially speaking. We often literally didn't know where the next meal was coming from, but we were happy as a family. Mr. Brown the Village Postmaster had a registered letter from Scotland with £5 in it awaiting us on arrival. We did Praise the Lord! Our ever-faithful God would meet our every need.

In those early days in Moulton, after we had been there a few months, Carolyn and Sharon started at the Village Primary School. Sharon was asked, as were other children in the beginners' class, "What did her father do for a living?" *No*, he was not a farmer, or a motor mechanic or a bricklayer. She replied instead, "He works for Jesus in the front room!" The teacher asked, "Why just the 'front room'?" It caused a chuckle!

Another incident from that period... Money was tight, but we never said anything to anybody. We did however commend our needs to God in prayer, and always paid our bills, living very simply. We used to have to pay the milk-lady each week. This naturally concerned Ann, my wife, because on one particular occasion, as we didn't have the money. Ann said, "You'll have to speak to her". "The Lord will provide," I said, "I'll tell her we will pay for two weeks' milk next week." The milk-lady said, "That will be fine" – she knew we were honest, and so we did pay her in full a week later.

This house recorded many interesting memories. Our dear Christian friend Alex, a bachelor, used to come for tea once a week on a Friday evening. Ann was (and is) very hospitable! A young Christian lady came to Northampton from Yorkshire to teach at the Barratt Maternity Hospital: she attended Grafton Square Evangelical Church, as we did, so Ann invited her to join us for tea. While we were enjoying the meal and their company Carolyn aged 7 years piped up, "When are you and Alex going to get married?" Ann and I didn't know where to put ourselves... But they did eventually get engaged and then married – so no harm was done. It might even have concentrated the mind!

Our first autumn in Moulton was indeed a testing time for us. We had to pay Lunn's the removal people £180 – in today's terms that would have been £800 or more. The £300 my grandmother had left me had almost all gone. The Lord in his wisdom had not supplied. What were we to do? The Bible says, "Owe no man any thing" (*Romans 13:8*). Payment was now urgent. Ann had an endowment policy that she cashed, sacrificially, and I had to go to London to pay off some of the bill with the cheque from this. It still left £90 outstanding.

God's Way Up Is Down
I could have taken the easy way out and obtained a full-time secular job, but then I would not have been able to carry on my all-important Gospel work among Mobile Home Park People. Jesus had said, and promised us:

> *Matthew 6:33* "But seek ye FIRST the kingdom of God, and His righteousness; and all these things shall be ADDED UNTO YOU."

How was the problem to be resolved?
At Moulton Secondary School they advertised for a part-time cleaner for the Autumn Term, three hours per evening. It was a very humble job to do and it took grace to apply for it. The Headmaster seemed to despise me for doing it. You see, *God's way up is down*. God despises the proud and gives grace to the humble. The Lord had a salient lesson to teach me:

51

this job still enabled me to carry on my evangelistic work, if a little restricted for a few months. But it gave a financial breathing space and the remaining £90 of the removal bill was soon paid. ***Praise God!***

A "Welcome" Message
After we had been in Moulton a few weeks the editor of 'The Moulton & Pitsford Baptist Magazine' (*Issue No 86, November 1967*) wrote:

Welcome

We warmly welcome Mr. & Mrs. Hector Hall and their little ones to our fellowship... Mr. Hall testifies to his Divine call to be an evangelist and to have special responsibility to taking the gospel to people who live in Mobile Homes. Too often such people are overlooked or neglected by the Churches of their district.

Christmas 1967
On Christmas Sunday 24th December 1967 I preached at Carey Baptist Church, Moulton, on *Isaiah 9:6*. This wonderful prophetic verse tells of the personal coming of Christ the Messiah, the Prince of Peace. Following the service, a local builder engaged me in conversation over the phrase,
"The government shall be upon His shoulder."

My understanding of it was that Isaiah was speaking of the Sovereignty of Christ ruling in world affairs. People were not unfriendly, but it was a more liberal Church, and Ann and I were looking for a distinctly Evangelical Church where the Word of God is expounded and the Gospel preached. Such a church was later to be found – as will be revealed in the next chapter. Also, at Christmas, I helped with the Christmas mail in the Northampton Drill Hall on "The Mounts". Because of my knowledge of the postal geography of Scotland, the Royal Mail put me on to sorting Scottish parcels!

19 The Aims and Principles of the Mission to Mobile Homes

In the early days in Moulton it was a bit of a struggle, as we had no car, and the Mobile Home Parks were mainly at some distance from our home. Nevertheless, we were very happy as a family, and Carolyn and Sharon were enjoying day school at Moulton County Primary. I spent time in the 'front room' – which we had painted a bright blue colour, having first removed three or four layers of wallpaper! As I spent time in prayer, waiting upon God, He confirmed the convictions already arrived at while we were in Scotland:

1. Evangelization of mobile home residents through personal evangelists.
2. That the MMH would be a FAITH PRINCIPLED Mission, with its DEPENDENCE UPON GOD. No appeals for money.

   We were confident that as long as we were faithfully preaching the Gospel of Christ and ministering to needy people, God would supply our every need.

   "My God shall supply all your need according to His riches in glory by Christ Jesus." *Philippians 4.19*
3. MISSION TITLE – 'THE MISSION TO MOBILE HOMES' – succinctly telling what its aims were.
4. MAGAZINE TITLE – 'FAITH & VICTORY' That was based on *1 John 5:4* "This is the victory that overcometh the world, even our faith."

I also decided to get a printed MAP of the British Isles, attached it to a chipboard 4 ft by 3 ft, and used black marker pins on it, to indicate the different Mobile Home Parks in England, Scotland and Wales. This helped in the way of Vision and prayer.

- Through this we could see progress being made, and people on Parks yet unreached by the gospel.
- Where we have already taken the gospel.

'Faith & VICTORY' – Victory, as St. Paul says in *1 Corinthians 15:57* "But thanks be to God, which giveth us the *Victory* through our Lord Jesus Christ." Yes, Satan would oppose such a spiritual ministry, but our Risen and VICTORIOUS LORD JESUS, who had conquered sin, death and Hell upon the Cross of Calvary would give the power of His Holy Spirit to complete the great task of evangelism among the many Mobile Home People.

They who know the Saviour shall in Him be strong.
Mighty in the conflict of the right 'gainst wrong;
This the blessed promise given in God's word,
Doing wondrous exploits, they who know the Lord

Chorus
Victory! victory! Blessed, blood-bought Victory!
Victory! Victory! Vict'ry all the time!
As Jehovah liveth, strength divine He giveth,

Unto those who know Him - vict'ry all the time!

Mrs. Leila Morris 1901

(**Note**: *Verse 3 ends, "Winning souls for Jesus, praise, O praise the Lord!" Amen, Amen: H.G.H.*)

Other important matters to do with the development of the Mission such as its Constitution, Basis of Faith etc. would follow once the Mission had its official inauguration, and its Council was formed.

A Church Discovered

After we had been in Moulton a week or so I prayed much for God's guidance and wisdom. A few weeks later, whilst in Northampton one day, I ventured to explore some of its streets on foot, like the Mounts, just off the centre of the town, and crossed over to Grafton Street: half-way down on the right my attention was drawn to the meeting place of the Grafton Square Evangelical Church – Minister, Rev. Brian Wilkinson. The Notice Board looked encouraging, and a note was made of the times of the Services. Thus at the first Sunday opportunity we went as a family to the church, and received an extremely warm welcome, and the ministry of Brian was distinctly Biblical.

There we made some sincere friendships, some of which last to the present day. Later the Church-Fellowship re-located to a new building North of the town, and Dr. Martyn Lloyd-Jones preached at the Opening Service. With the new location, the name changed to Reynard Way Evangelical Church (F.I.E.C.). We cannot speak too highly of the help given to us as a family by Tom (a Deacon) and Dorothy Simpson. They took us to their hearts, and as we didn't have a car in those early days, they gave us a lift to Church each Sunday, and were given to hospitality. When I was away preaching or evangelizing they always looked after Ann, Carolyn and Sharon, as our own families were far away in Essex and in Scotland. They were the proverbial 'Salt of the earth'.

We started a Monthly Prayer Meeting in our home for the work of the MMH, and they and others faithfully supported it. So God answered our prayers. Praise His name!

A Little Bit About Northampton –
and Some Notable Christians.

Northampton, "as every schoolboy knows", was famous for its shoe industry. It even made shoes for King John (and his army) – however, I don't know what size of shoe he wore. On the Christian front there are a few notable names associated with Northampton and its environs, such as **William Carey** (1761-1834), the pioneer missionary to India and a great Bible translator, who began work as an apprentice cobbler.

Philip Doddridge (1702-51), who had a Theological Academy in the town, wrote such well-known hymns as "O Happy Day, That Fixed My Choice" (on Thee, my Saviour and my God). He ministered at The Independent Chapel in Gold Street and helped in the beginning of The General Hospital.

In more recent times **John P. Williamson** C.B.E. K.P.M. (King's Police Medal award), who came originally from Cumbria, made his name while Chief Constable of Northamptonshire. He belonged to the Open Brethren, and my friend Alex Adkins suggested that I pay him a visit at his home near the Golf Course. He was by then retired from Police service, having in 1948 helped to re-organize the Israel Police Force. He graciously received me, his wife made me a cup of tea, and good fellowship was enjoyed. He knew personally Mr. John Neville Knox, our MMH Vice-President at that time, and who like himself was a keen 'Gideon'. He showed interest in evangelism among the Mobile Home people, and he revealed his great love for the Lord Jesus and was a keen student of the Word of God*. He encouraged me, and we always had prayer always before I left. We thank God for such distinguished men of God who serve Him in their generation.

* One of his favourite texts was *Proverbs 22:29*: "Seest thou a man diligent in his business? He shall stand before kings; he shall not stand before mean *(margin - obscure)* men."

How true that was of his life.

20   The MMH Inaugural Meeting

The Mission's Inaugural Meeting took place at **King's Cross Baptist Church Hall** by kind permission, on Friday 13th September 1968. The following were present:

Peter C. Assheton	**Wilfred E. Boggis**
Brian L. Morphew	**H. Peter Rawlings**
Hector G. Hall	

Hector had been very active in evangelizing the residents of Mobile Home Parks in Scotland and Northamptonshire, and a few in Essex and Surrey for the past year and three months.

Mr. P.C. Assheton was appointed Chairman. He had been a fellow-member – with Hector – at Hoddeston Baptist Church, and was a lecturer at the College of Law, Guildford.

Mr. Wilfred E. Boggis was in Insurance, with F.I.E.C connections, and was concerned that the new Mission should have a Scriptural Basis of Faith, and that new workers and Council Members should affirm it annually.

Mr. Brian L. Morphew was a fellow member of Grafton Square Evangelical Church (later Reynard Way Evangelical Church), Northampton, and was Chief Careers Officer for Northampton. He was appointed Minute Secretary.

Last, but not least, **Mr. H. Peter Rawlings**, an Evangelical Anglican with keen Missionary interest, and in Banking by profession, was appointed Honorary Treasurer. His mother Mrs. Julia Rawlings and her sister Mrs. Pennington were keen prayer-partners of this fledging Mission.

Mr. Hall read from the Scriptures, and made a brief statement concerning his call in to the work. Hector had a God-given passion to reach these forgotten people with the Saving Gospel of Christ.

Other Practical Matters – taken from the Minutes of the Meeting.

Specimen Signatures for Savings Bank account.
Mr. Rawlings proposed, and Mr. Boggis seconded, that the Director, Treasurer, and one other Council member be authorized. Messrs Hall, Morphew and Rawlings were duly authorized.

Constitution
It was agreed that Mr. Hall should prepare a draft Constitution in consultation with members of the Council for consideration at the next Meeting. This would include a **Doctrinal Basis** (see **Appendix 1**).

Development of the work
Mr. Hall stated that there were promising developments at Caravan Sites in Bedfordshire, Essex and Scotland. There was to be a follow-up in Scotland shortly.

Future Calling of other evangelists
Mr. Hall stated that there were approximately 100 known Mission supporters (i.e. Prayer Partners), and 220 copies of the 'Faith & Victory' Prayer Letter were being circulated at that present time. Two Churches

were assisting in the financial support – Beith Mission, Scotland, and Grafton Square Evangelical Free Church, Northampton. The pattern of working was in prayer, in making contacts on Caravan Parks and in follow-up. "Faith & Victory" was at present circulated at the Bible Training Institute, Glasgow and Birmingham Bible Institute, and there was contact with the Bible College of Wales. It was suggested that circulation might also be made to All Nations Christian College and to London Bible College.

Sundry Requirements
A Ledger and Minute Book to be purchased from existing funds in the Savings Bank account, which amounted to £8-0-0d. Mr. Boggis agreed to approach persons known to him who could assist in designing a printed letterhead, and in printing. Mr. Morphew agreed to arrange for the Minutes to be circulated to the Council, prior to the next meeting. Mr. Assheton suggested that it might be worthwhile to make enquiries regarding the installation of a telephone, without entering into any obligation at this stage.

Any other business
Mr. Hall asked to continue to be known by the term 'Director' as at present, to combine in one word the function of evangelist and secretary. Mr. Assheton proposed and Mr. Morphew seconded the formal appointment of the Rev. Andrew MacBeath as President of the Mission, and Mr. J. Neville Knox as Vice President. In both eases it had been signified to Mr. Hall that they accepted his invitation to serve in these capacities.

The Meeting closed in prayer at 8.50 p.m.

Signed: *P.C. Assheton*
2nd November '68.

Postscript
Hector travelled back by train to Northampton with our brother Brian Morphew – arriving after midnight – so excited and thankful to God for significant progress made in the founding of '**The Mission to Mobile Homes**'.

21 Many Interesting People Met

In the early days in evangelism on the Northamptonshire mobile home parks our resources were limited. A few Parks were near to our home in

Moulton, but many others were at a distance. It was all a learning process, but we were conscious that God was at work, and that His Holy Spirit would guide and direct.

My 'Caravan Sites Handbook' came to my aid again and again in locating different M. H. Parks within reach of home. At Burton Latimer, home of Weetabix, the famous breakfast cereal, there was in the centre of the village a small residential M. H. Park, interestingly next to the Baptist Chapel.

In this Park I met a fine Gypsy family by the name of – yes, you've guessed it – Smith! (Incidentally, most of the people on the park were not Gypsies.) At that time the Smith family lived in a small four-berth Caravan tucked away in the corner. They must have heard on Sundays the hymn singing from the Chapel nearby. But strangely, there seemed to be little if any contact by the Chapel people. The family was made up of Dad – Jack – who did tar-macadam work for a living, a truly hard-working man, and Mum Edna, who kept the home beautifully clean. Their son Shane, then about 8 or 9 years of age, attended the local Primary School, and in a year or two would pass the 'Eleven Plus' examination and attend Kettering Grammar School, and their daughter was little Debra. At the Primary School when something went missing Shane was wrongly accused, just because he was from a Gypsy family.

I was warmly welcomed into their home, and freely read the Scriptures and explained the Way of Salvation through the shed blood of Christ upon the Cross, and prayer was offered for God's blessing on the family. This initial contact led to openings among the Gypsy folk in that part of the county.

My visit to Towcester residential Caravan Park was quite different. I took two buses, the first to Northampton and then a second bus on to Towcester. On the first visit I was refused permission to visit the people – I can't remember after all these years what the excuse was. Later, through prayer and persistence, God opened the door, as He did in later years on other parks where permission to visit was not initially granted. And so on this Park I was then enabled to share the Gospel of Christ with a number of people, and to leave Christian literature. In particular I remember 'Leana', a senior citizen. When she said to me, "My heart is broken", it was my joy to tell her of JESUS who came to heal the "broken hearted".

Isaiah 61:1 "The Spirit of the Lord God is upon me; …He hath sent me to bind up the broken hearted."

Prayer was had with her, and kindness was shown to her on follow-up visits.

Also, I remember a one-parent family who didn't have much, and I could only give the Mum sweets for the children for Christmas. Our Christmas Cheer work was to come into action later. It has not been my policy to tell what gifts I give to people. Jesus says:

> *Matthew 6:3* "But when thou doest alms *(give gifts)*, let not thy left hand know what thy right hand doeth."

The background was the hypocritical stance of the Pharisees. Gifts given later in the Mission's name are different. All gifts given are for God's glory.

In the early days in Moulton, when mobility was limited, I used the pen 'that is mightier than the sword':

Letter to the ***Sunday Companion*** 30th December 1967.

THE RIGHT HOUSE

We were interested to read in "Personally Speaking" of how God guided you to the right house to buy. We too, have recently had a similar experience of God's goodness in providing a three-bedroom house to rent in Moulton, although at the time we resided in Scotland.

As a matter of interest, we are engaged in evangelism among mobile home dwellers and needed somewhere more central in Britain as a base, as well as a home! I have personally taken the Gospel to residential caravan dwellers in parks across the central lowlands of Scotland – from Ayr to Edinburgh – and in the North of England.

The Lord has wonderfully blessed in restoring back-sliders, saving souls and starting new Sunday Schools.

This ministry is continuing during the winter, and mobile home residents in Northamptonshire and Bedfordshire are being challenged to repent and believe the Gospel.

We value readers' prayers.

With kind regards, Hector & Ann Hall, Moulton.

WHATEVER THE WEATHER
Christian Herald, January 20ᵗʰ 1968.

Each evening local farmers and others wait in the Moulton village newsagents for the evening paper. Whatever the weather – rain, wind or snow – they are there.

We Christians should have the same earnest desire for the good news of the Word of God, and meditate upon it daily, and attend public exposition, as did the Christians at Berea:

Acts 17:11 "These were more noble than those in Thessalonica, in that they received the word with all readiness of mind, and searched the Scriptures daily, whether those things were so."

Moulton, Northants.   HECTOR G. HALL

Northampton Chronicle & Echo, December 7ᵗʰ 1967
CHALLENGE

It was very refreshing to read in "Pilgrim's Report" (Chronicle and Echo, December 1ˢᵗ 1967) of the Rev. Arundel Barker's challenge to the teenagers of Deanshanger to "have guts" and attend his evening services for six consecutive Sundays.

Jesus Christ commenced His public ministry with a challenge to "repent and believe the Gospel" – a revolutionary note which too often is absent from our pulpits today, with disastrous results.

Hector G. Hall, 1 Prince of Wales Row, Moulton.

---

22   My Memories of Bellshill
Psalm 148:8 "Stormy wind fulfilling His word."

In the Summer of 1967 I visited residential Caravan Parks across Central Scotland. This included the one situated in the centre of Bellshill, near the Swimming Pool.   Bellshill is a town 10 miles east of Glasgow. On this Park I met, amongst others, a spiritually back-slidden Salvation Army couple. I tried to help the young man to return to the Lord, in the reading of God's word and with prayer.

On the 15ᵗʰ of January 1968 there was a terrible storm across Central Scotland with winds reaching 130 miles per hour. A newspaper headline for that day recorded that in Scotland: "Hurricane force gales cause 20

Deaths". This young couple were by now blessed with a baby girl, and at the height of the storm the mother left the baby in the Caravan to get help. For some reason the husband wasn't there – I don't know why – perhaps he was at work. Anyway, after she left the caravan and her baby, the caravan got blown away by the fierceness of this very powerful storm. When she returned, the caravan had literally disintegrated, but providentially the baby was found – fast asleep! Amazingly God in HIS Mercy had protected and preserved the child against great odds. Praise God! The husband told me this story upon my next visit there at Easter 1968, up from Northampton (where God had led my family and I to live the previous October). So severe had been the storm that solid stone gables on Glasgow tenements were blown off. I later saw the effects with my own eyes.

In September of that same year (1968) Bellshill Baptist Church gave me the opportunity to show a coloured slide presentation of 'Evangelism of the Mobile Home Parks across Central Scotland' – from Ayr to Edinburgh. This informed the congregation and encouraged prayer. Many people didn't know that a lot of these sites existed, and were thrilled that GOD was AT WORK amongst them. Their minister Rev. Campbell and his wife graciously invited me to tea prior to that meeting, and gave me hospitality overnight, which was appreciated. It was a memorable night, in more ways than one…

Rev. Campbell told me how the Committee of Ministers had, after considerable thought and prayer, chosen the word "TELL" (Scotland) to describe the Billy Graham Crusade (from *St. Mathew's Gospel Chapter 28 verses 7, 9 & 10*). Rev. Campbell, as well as his pastoral ministry, lectured on the subject of 'Antiques', and was an authority on that subject. He put me in a large room in which I was down to sleep. In there were numerous clocks of all descriptions, chiming on the hour, quarter-past the hour, half past the hour, quarter to the hour etc., etc.! Needless to say, "Yours truly" found it a hard job to sleep that night, and did not get to sleep to 2.30am in the morning. To my amazement at 5.30am the door opened and in came Rev. Mr. Campbell with a tray of breakfast porridge, toast and marmalade, and a pot of tea (he was a Highland man). What a short night!

Finally, Mrs. Campbell was famous for her love of cats (many rescued) – she had nine at this time. Each time I came home from visiting the Manse, Ann said she could smell the cats, and knew where I had been. Sadly – many years later – this dear man of God, now elderly, was knocked down and killed on the main road trying to save the life of a dog. So we "thank God" for His dear servant, now with Christ in Heaven.

23   My First Visit to Newport, Gwent, South Wales

From the 'Caravan Sites' handbook details were obtained of the residential sites in Newport, Gwent. So after much prayer and thought I set forth for Newport. As the coach travelled through the Cotswolds *via* Cheltenham, where a change of coach had to be made, I prayed much for God to guide me and to provide for me a bed for the night. I didn't know a soul in the area then, in late November 1968.

It was high risk strategy, as on arrival in Newport there would be just about 30-40 minutes before it got dark. On leaving the Bus Station at Newport my direction took me north of the town; I walked up Stow Hill and on the right-hand side near the top I obtained a bed for one night in a small hotel – all that my finances really allowed. It was providential that I took that route, because on the left-hand side going up was a small Elim Church (now alas occupied by the Muslims). Also, in the will of God there was a meeting there that very evening, where an elderly Christian couple Mr. and Mrs. B. very kindly offered to give me hospitality for the next couple of nights, while I did Gospel outreach. Praise God! Their fellowship and hospitality were spontaneously offered and greatly appreciated. My heart was full of praise to God as I returned to the hotel that night, and the next morning I found my way over to Mr. and Mrs. B's home on the other side of the city.

A brief reconnaissance of the area was made, as best I could. Thus I found the Pye Corner Caravan Park, and commenced to share the Gospel of Christ with people from one caravan to another, as was my custom, leaving copies of *"Emergency Post"*. However, the rain became so heavy that I couldn't continue visiting since no one invited me in, and the strong wind was blowing my umbrella from pillar to post – it was tough.

Mr. & Mrs. B.'s fellowship was much appreciated that evening, and I wrote to Ann. On reflection, this was a foothold in South Wales, but only a foothold: but one that later was to result in real blessing. God who is ever in control was, unknown to us, about to send a Christian couple from my own Church (Hoddesdon Baptist Church) to live in Newport! These were Mr. Ian and Mrs. Judy Walker, who would for over 30 years give me friendship, fellowship and hospitality while in South Wales. Nant Coch Church and Lliswerry Road Baptist Church, both in Newport, were also later to support the work of the MMH.

On the last morning of that first visit Ann's letter arrived with the sad news of our Sharon's accident back in Moulton. It is included here with its personal contents, as it reveals what it costs evangelists and their wives to be parted the one from the other, on the King's business, when their children are young. Sharon would have been 2½ years old and Carolyn 5 years old at that time. (*As I have read this letter once again, 50 or so years later, – it has brought tears to my eyes. H.H.*)

> *1 Prince of Wales Row,*
> *Moulton, Northampton*
> *Wed 27ᵗʰ Nov. '68*

Dear Hector

Thank you for your letter yesterday morning and this morning. I'm glad you've got fixed up with some where to stay....

I am wondering Hector if you could definitely come home on Friday (D.V.) because I've to take Sharon to the hospital on Saturday morning. I'm sorry to say we've been in trouble again.

Yesterday taking Carolyn to school, Sharon had an accident (I'll give you all the details when you come home).

The outcome of it was I had to take her to Hospital (Northampton General) and get stitches in her forehead. She was very good and everybody was helpful… Sharon is much better now, but I've to take her again on Saturday to see how the stitches are and if they are ready to come out. Poor little thing she's in trouble. Looking forward to seeing you on Friday D.V.

> *All my love,*
>
> *Ann*

The wee ones send their love.   (Sharon's scribbles!)

P.S. I learned lessons from this early experience:

Firstly, November was not the best month to be away from home to do pioneer evangelism on the Residential Caravan Parks.

Secondly, and more importantly, it was not the ideal time to be away from my young wife and young family. Better to be working locally to home at this time of the year when the weather was at its worst, and the evenings dark.

In the following years, I usually went to South Wales in late May when the weather was good – see the sequel in later chapters. We saw God's wonderful out-working in witnessing to Christ the only Saviour of sinners on Mobile Home Parks from Newport to Swansea.

24   Two 1968 reports by Hector G Hall, MMH Director

1 – Sowing the Seed in Surrey

Psalm 126:6 He that goeth forth and weepeth, bearing precious seed, shall doubtless come again with rejoicing.

We give praise to God for a memorable week (27th July to 3rd August 1968) of evangelism and deputation in the Guildford area of Surrey. Seven residential Caravan Parks were visited with the Gospel, in the surrounding villages of Shalford, Chilworth, Wood Street, Worplesdon, Normandy and Ash.

At Shalford on a relatively new park being developed I met a lady who said she regularly received the *"Emergency Post"* from a Christian friend at Abinger. "Not interested," remarked a man in an abrupt manner, when encouraged to turn to God and to know Christ as his personal Saviour. A young Jewish lady was asked if she had ever read the prophecy of *Isaiah 53* and she replied, "No". So, I read from *verses 3-6*, "He is despised and rejected of men... All we like sheep have gone astray; we have turned every one to his own way; and the Lord hath laid on Him the iniquity of us all", and told how these prophetic verses speak clearly of Jesus Christ.

On another Park situated by the river at Shalford I encountered a Scotsman from Perth who thanked me for calling. Also, a lady who was gardening listened to the good seed of the Word of God and was pleased to be given a Gospel of St. John. A family living in one of the houseboats invited me in. He was a French Roman Catholic and she an English Anglican. After listening to their experiences – over a cup of coffee – I then had the opportunity to present the redeeming love of Christ, for them. Earlier in the year this dear man had been in hospital in Gloucester and a Christian minister had visited him – so we are all links in the Divine chain.

On a small Caravan Park at Wood Street, four boys gathered round and listened to the story of Zacchaeus, who received Jesus joyfully. They were given copies, of *"Our Treasury"* which contains the Word of God, and Bible quizzes, etc., for them to do at home, and they were encouraged to attend Sunday School.

At Normandy I met a woman who remembered my visit last year. In one of the new Mobile Homes I came across a lady who was very lonely. She had moved there in April and did not know any one. I read *Psalm 46* and told her of the Lord Jesus, who is a faithful friend and Saviour, and prayer was offered. She has since been sent a Church magazine, and her name has been passed on to Guildford Baptist Church, who have promised to follow up with her and with other contacts made.

On an adjoining site a man was contacted, who has a police record – we met last year. He was clean-shaven and smartly dressed, but further away from God. He said, "Christianity is rubbish". I handed him a tract: "Perhaps this may be a help to you". He rudely replied "I shall put this down the W.C." and he quickly shut the door. He needs our prayers. Good fellowship was enjoyed with two of the Lord's people at Worplesdon Caravan Park.

A woman at Ash (near Aldershot) said, "The Church and me aren't the best of friends". I questioned: "What about God and you?" She answered, "Perhaps when we meet up there", pointing heavenward. I answered, "Only in this life can we turn to God".

We take this opportunity of thanking Mr. Peter Assheton, Acting-Chairman of The Mission to Mobile Homes, for arranging deputation meetings at Guildford Baptist Church (Commercial Road) in conjunction with Mr. P. Boreham, Church Secretary; at Ward Street Hall in conjunction with Professor Waldron, and at the College of Law Christian Fellowship, which informed Christian people of this ministry, and encouraged prayer. We also thank Peter and Marion for their fellowship in the furtherance of the Gospel, their kind hospitality, and transport to and from Moulton. We return praise to the LORD for His faithfulness and goodness to us, and we thank all who have a share in this vital ministry by their prayers and gifts.

Monthly Prayer Meetings

BEITH, Ayrshire, Scotland.　　　1st Friday at 7.30 p.m. Secretary - Mrs. M. Kirkwood, 13 Mains Road.

MOULTON, Northants.　　　2nd Friday at 7.30 p.m.

Mr. & Mrs. H. Hall, 1 Prince of Wales Row.

2 – Consolidation and Extension in Scotland

1 Corinthians 15:58 "Be ye stedfast, unmoveable, always abounding in the work of the Lord".

Let me record a few of the highlights of my ten-day (20th to 30th September 1968) Evangelistic and Deputation Tour of Central Scotland, which was blessed of God, to whom we offer praise.

At Nivensknowe Park, Loanhead, I said farewell to Dr. Hey on the Monday and wondered who would take over the Sunday School, carry on a testimony to our Lord and Saviour, and teach the children the Word of God. When I first came there in July 1967, there were nine committed Christians; now they have all moved away: Mr. & Mrs. Alex Brady and Dr. Hey being the last to go.

However, prayer prevailed and visitation continued on the Tuesday morning and thus I came across a young Irish Baptist couple, David and Anna Bowers, who had been led there by the Lord two months previously – unknown to us – and they have both taught in a Sunday School and are keen to serve the Lord, so the Sunday School resumed on 3rd November in their own mobile home, under their leadership. This incident reminded us afresh that this is the Lord's work. He has His hand upon it.

Significantly, David and Anna Bowers told me of our brother Tom Meaney, who was at that time Superintendent of Skipton Street Baptist Mission, East Belfast. This led to God opening the door to Gospel outreach on the Caravan Parks in Northern Ireland and deputation opportunities there for the MMH. Details of the first meeting and impressions of 8th April 1970 will appear in a later Chapter.

The principle given in *Acts 1:8* was beginning to work out: Scotland, England, Wales and then Northern Ireland.

> *Acts 1:8* "But ye shall receive power, after that the Holy Ghost is come upon you: and ye shall be witnesses unto Me both in Jerusalem, and in all Judaea, and in Samaria, and unto the uttermost part of the earth."

[Incidentally, David and Ann were later (in 1980) called of God to serve Christ with I.B.F.M. (Irish Baptist Foreign Mission) as missionaries in Peru. They served for some time in Tacna, where Ann Hall, née Creighton, was born. Ann's parents Bill and Helen Creighton also served faithfully with the same Mission.]

People were also followed up on Pentland Caravan Park at Loanhead, and at Bellshill, Lanarkshire. We give praise to God that the outreach has been extended to Caravan Parks, at Little France, Edinburgh, and at Port Seton. At Little France I explained to a man on the Park that "I wished to visit the people on this park and encourage, them to have faith in God, and know Christ as a living Saviour." He replied with a chuckle, "You don't find many who are that way nowadays: certainly not here".

One lady with a Church of Scotland background said that she "had lost faith in the Church, but not in God". These people need our prayers.

At Port Seton on the Firth of Forth, a refined middle-aged lady told me she went to Church, but she did not know Jesus Christ as a personal Saviour. I read *John's Gospel 1:10-12* and *3:16*, and she seemed definitely interested and accepted this Gospel to read for herself.

On Saturday afternoon Duncan Black (our West of Scotland representative) and I visited Erskine Ferry and Westferry Mobile Home Parks. The Lord gave us openings. A Roman Catholic lady listened to the Gospel with much interest and was pleased to receive a John's Gospel, as she did not possess a Bible. It was a real joy to see Duncan visit a number of these homes on his own, commending Christ, while I visited others. We ask our readers to pray for Duncan, as he visits these Parks on his own in the future.

A complete stranger very kindly gave us a lift in his car – answered prayer, as there were no buses – from Erskine Hospital to Langbank, and showed much interest in our work. He listened to my testimony *en route* and said he was a church-goer but had not had such an experience. We reminded him before leaving that "Now is the accepted time; behold now is the day of Salvation" *2 Corinthians 6:2*. Duncan and I felt God had led us to this young man.

On the Westferry Caravan Park, I introduced Duncan to the owner and his wife, and to a number of other people, including a middle-aged man, an agnostic, whom I had met before. He said he was "not interested", refused to take a copy of the *'Emergency Post'*, and quickly cut the conversation short. It reminded us that people today, as in Jeremiah's day, "reject the Word of the Lord."

25 Outreach in the Border Area and Central Scotland

*The following reports are taken, **substantially verbatim**, from the July 1969 issue of "FAITH & VICTORY", the MMH Newsletter*

*They show the extended outreach by MMH evangelists in the **Border Area** and **Central Scotland** at that time.*

Proclaiming the Saviour around Solway Firth Mobile Home Parks

By H. G. Hall

It is with praise in my heart to the Lord that I pen this report of Gospel outreach to Caravan dwellers on six Parks from Workington, Cumberland to Dumfries, Scotland. Over two hundred people heard the message of Salvation in Christ (24th to 31st May 1969).

On the journey to Carlisle I sat down in the train opposite a Christian lady and through the disturbance of a drunken man I gave up my seat – all part of God's plan – for later on I sat down in a different compartment opposite a Jewish playboy and gambler. He opened his heart to me and told me he was "living for this life." I asked him what future had he? What about eternity? He replied, "When you are dead, you are dead". I told him Christ died on the cross for our sins, according to the Scriptures, and that He was buried and rose again, and that we need to prepare for eternity. He told me a converted Jew had spoken to him in Manchester. He listened with interest to my testimony of Christ's saving grace and said he would read the Gospel of St. John given to him.

At Allonby, Mr. J. Pattinson of the Cumberland Scripture Trust and I visited a large Holiday Caravan Park, and we were led of God to a man whom Mr. Pattinson had not seen for 42 years. He had worked in the pit with Mr. Pattinson when he was 15 years of age. Then followed a dialogue of their lives since, and Mr. Pattinson briefly told him that he had been 40 years in the Lord's service in Cumberland. It was good having fellowship with our brother, who is doing a good work.

On a Mobile Home Park in a beautiful setting on the outskirts of Workington I met a saved man, now retired, who delights to read the Word of God daily. Each home was visited and Christian literature distributed.

The Lord answered prayer concerning Newbridge Caravan Park (Dumfries) as this community has been on my heart for some time. I met a young man who was quick to state he regularly attends the Church of Scotland, but when asked if he knew Jesus Christ as his own personal Saviour and Lord, could not answer in the affirmative. So often God the Holy Spirit is preparing hearts. For example, Mrs. W., who had recently lost her father, was very pleased to hear the message of Salvation in Christ. She gladly accepted a Scripture Gift Mission booklet explaining the Way of Salvation, and thanked me for calling.

At Gretna I went specifically to see a girl who went there from the Midlands to got married and stayed on. Her mother had asked me to call. She had actually moved on to another Park, and I was able to visit her and pass on her mother's good wishes and remind her of God's love for her.

Edward Hodgson came with me on my second visit to Silloth Lido residential Park and this was all to the good as he is a member of the Silloth Mission, and we were able to invite people to the services. We met a mathematics student who revealed that he had tried three denominations but had not yet come to personal saving faith in Christ. He says his prayers at night. He is seeking. He listened to my testimony with real interest. We also visited a Holiday Park, and had a long conversation with a Roman Catholic man, opened the Word of God and read *John 3:16*, and left him with that Gospel to read. We take this opportunity of thanking Edward and Averil Hodgson for their gracious hospitality and help in arranging meetings in Cumberland. Praise God and pray for all mentioned above, and those whom we haven't space to mention.

Rev. Andrew MacBeath

Our beloved President retired in June after 14 years as Principal, of the Bible Training Institute, Glasgow.

We thank God for Mr. MacBeath's Christ-like life, missionary vision, and faithful teaching of the Word of God which have influenced the lives of countless B.T.I. students throughout the world.

We pray that he may have a blessed and fruitful retirement.

Soul Winning in Scotland

(2nd to 21st April)

Proverbs 11:30 "He that winneth souls is wise."

We give praise to God for almost three weeks evangelistic ministry across central Scotland from Gourock to Edinburgh, and from Lanark in the south to Perth in the North, in fellowship with Associate Evangelists, Duncan Black and Alex Marshall. We followed up people on five Mobile Home Parks and the residents of four new Parks were visited with the Gospel. I was concerned to follow up people contacted on previous, visits and to introduce them to Mr. Black, who is personally concerned with sites on the West of Scotland. At the Cloch Park we met a middle-aged woman whom Mr. Hall had met before. She revealed that she was seeking after the Lord and had been reading the New Testament, and takes her little girl to an undenominational Sunday School "where she can learn the message of the Bible."

At Wemyss Bay we met a man visiting friends who was particularly interested in spiritual matters. He was a little confused in his thinking. He thought that the "resurrection" meant "being born again". We explained that Jesus said, "Ye must be born again" of the Holy Spirit, in this life. Duncan testified to the fact that he had had a personal experience of Salvation when he was nine years of age. He had made a definite choice. I too gave my testimony of the saving grace of God and he asked, "How do you know you are forgiven?" We felt led to this man, as he told us a Christian at his business had invited him and his fiancée to St. Georges Tron Church in Glasgow. His fiancée seemed to be the stumbling block. Please pray that he may put Christ first, and that both he and his fiancée may be saved.

In the providence of God Mr. Marshall was able to take a week's holiday, and he very kindly escorted me in his car to all the places where I had deputation Meetings, and we were able to reach out to new Parks with the Gospel. This gave. Mr. Marshall an introduction to our methods of visitation evangelism, and before long he was visiting on his own. Mrs. Marshall also assisted with gracious hospitality in their home at Bathgate.

We visited Rumfort Caravan Park, Stirlingshire, where, we were well received by the owner who gave us permission to visit the homes. The first one that we went to was occupied by a young married woman who was a schoolteacher. She teaches the children for a period of religious instruction, yet only accepts that our Lord is a dead historical figure. We presented the living Christ to her, Who died for our sins, and was buried and rose again. We pray that she may think again. The Lord gave Alex the opportunity to speak to a Roman Catholic lady who had lost four children. He was able to tell her of his own loss of faith through a similar experience, and how God had given him peace and comfort that no man or church could give.

We also visited Clyde Valley Caravan Park. In this beautiful setting you could feel the presence of the Creator. Mr. and Mrs. R. were encountered. Mr. R. was aggressive when we called because he thought we were from a false cult, but when he realised we were genuine Christians his attitude changed and he informed us that his wife was a Christian and invited us into his home, where we enjoyed a short time of fellowship. The old lady was thrilled at being able to chat and have prayer with fellow Christians.

At Glencarse, near Perth, the Roman Catholic lady who owns the site listened to the message of the Gospel and was very co-operative. We were led of the Lord to a particular home where a young couple are searching for an answer to their spiritual and physical problems. Unfortunately, they were receiving regular instruction from a false cult. We spent some time with this young couple explaining the true way to faith through our Lord and Saviour Jesus Christ. Do pray for this family, particularly the little baby daughter who lies in a Perth Hospital in poor health.

The final Gospel Meeting at Polmadie Railway Mission, Glasgow, was a memorable one as people in the street were invited to the meeting. Eleven teenagers did attend and Christ was uplifted (*John12:32*) through the Holy Spirit's power, and a Roman Catholic fellow 13 years of age was counselled after the meeting. Please pray for this young man.

All praise to God, who answers prayer.

26   A Story from the "Garden of England"

In August 1969 God provided, through a kind friend at Tollington Park Baptist Church, London, for the Hall family to have a good fortnight's holiday at their lovely holiday bungalow on the Isle of Sheppey – just off the Kent coast. Indeed, a great kindness - how good is the God we adore! Together with Ann, Carolyn, then aged six years, and Sharon, aged three-and-a-half, we had a lovely holiday there. But on the Thursday, I prayed and planned whilst in the area to visit the High View

Estate Mobile Home Park at Harvel (approximately ten miles from Gravesend) to personally bring the Saving message of Christ.

A man who kindly gave me a lift from Minster on the Isle of Sheppey – he was going to Gravesend – especially went out of his way to get me to Harvel, all of his own volition. God was at work. *En route* my Gospel errand would no doubt have been explained. "After enquiring at 3 petrol stations and 1 fire station we eventually arrived at the village called Harvel." So read the report at the time.

At the entrance to the Park I met a lady by the name of Mrs. Weymouth, who turned out to be a Christian and she informed me of two Christian brothers – who were butchers by profession – and who kindly took her and her husband to church on a Sunday in their car.

Two Jehovah's Witnesses were contacted and the Gospel presented. A young man from Zambia – recently arrived in England – listened to the Gospel. At one of the last homes visited a Pentecostal lady invited me in to her home. She had not long been converted and was undergoing a time of trial and testing, so I opened my Bible and read:
> *1 Peter 1:7* "That the trial of your faith, being much more precious than gold that perisheth, though it be tried with fire, might be found unto praise and honour and glory at the appearing of Jesus Christ."

Such trial of faith is precious because it refines us like silver and gold. God allows it to strengthen our faith and make us more like the Lord Jesus. We then had prayer for God to strengthen her by His Word and Holy Spirit. As I left she said, "You have made my day. My spirit has been lifted high. PRAISE GOD!" He sent me there: to whom be all Praise and glory.

On walking the two-and-a-half miles to the station through the beautiful garden of England my eyes caught sight of fields of wheat – "Golden and ripe for harvest". My prayer was: *"Oh God, send forth labourers into this needy Harvest Field. In Jesus' name. Amen."*

Just imagine a community of some eight hundred people living in the countryside miles from anywhere. We greatly enjoyed our holiday with the sea, sand and all of God's wonderful Creation, with good weather and fellowship on the Lord's Day with God's people at the Islands Baptist Churches.

A Practical Problem
After ten days our food and money ran out. You see, our resources (of God's supply) so often came by letter i.e. the postman, and people didn't know where we were staying. We didn't have credit cards in those days, and it was our custom not to get into debt. However, we did see God's provision in different ways and in particular the blackberries on the hedgerows and the apples put in boxes at the front gate of houses with the words "Please Help Yourself"! So, we eventually returned home having had a lovely holiday in the county known as the *Garden of England*.

A Sequel
The two brothers mentioned earlier were from Meopham Green. Not only were they butchers, but one of them was Secretary of Assembly Hall Baptist Church (name since changed). He arranged for me to preach there on the Lord's Day 15th March 1970, and report on Gospel ministry among Mobile Home People. They appreciated the ministry of God's Word and the Gospel of Christ, and were very kind to me giving gracious hospitality and a generous ministry gift – and to top it all a good Lamb Joint and sausages! *"He doeth all things well."* Thank God for Christian butchers!

Finally, many years later I heard the same man being interviewed on BBC2 *"Down Your Way"* programme coming from Meopham Green. I can't now remember his name – but Heaven records such kindness.

27   Blessings and Bombs in Belfast
6th – 10th April 1970

Tim Hames – *"The Times"* January 29th 2007: *"For the better part of 30 years a corner of the United Kingdom was riven by the most brutal civil unrest experienced by any part of Western Europe in the 20th century"*.

In almost every year of that traumatic period I visited Belfast on evangelistic and deputation work with the MMH.

How Did I First Come to Go to Belfast?
In 1969 Mr. and Mrs. David and Anna Bowers, leaders of the MMH Sunday School on the Pentland Park, Loanhead, told me of Tom and Irene Meaney, leaders of Skipton Street Baptist Mission in East Belfast. We prayed, and they invited me to come over and speak at the Mission. Thus it was in early May 1970 that I first came to Belfast, this historic Protestant city. Much prayer preceded the journey, getting a Burns & Laird Lines ferry from Adrossan to Belfast (as I was traveling from

Scotland) leaving at 10am and arriving at 2.15pm. A beautiful sail across the Irish Sea, with good weather! The Lord was very gracious, because on board the ferry was Rev. and Mrs. Henson of the Church of Nazarene, Irvine. It was good to have fellowship with fellow-believers. It was a lovely journey up the Belfast Lough into Donegal Quay, where Tom and Irene met me.

First Impressions and First Meeting

The beautiful Granite City Hall, with its magnificent dome, is situated at the centre of the City, and is impressive. Its walls got tarnished during the 'troubles' but have since been re-cleaned. The giant Harland & Wolf "Goliath and Samson" cranes dominate the skyline of the city of the "Titanic". Tom and Irene and Peter made me feel quite at home. On arrival at Skipton Street, there were buntings and red, white and blue Union Jacks were to be seen along the road and across the street. It was like V.E. Day all over again! We had an encouraging meeting, with a message from Scripture, and a Coloured Slide presentation of "Evangelism Among Caravan Dwellers".

First Ulster Mobile Home Park Visited

My first visit to a Northern Ireland Park was at Knocknagoney. I had boarded an Ulster bus at The Arches, Bloomfield, intending to go to Bangor and Groomsport. But as we passed along the Knocknagoney Road I saw the **Orchard Residential Park** and I immediately got off. As the Park Office was closed I commenced outreach, not knowing that the majority of residents of this small park were Jehovah's Witnesses. However, I did meet one lady who was a Baptist, and had good fellowship with her. I learnt that one of her neighbours was a gentleman who claimed to be one of the so-called 144,000, as mentioned in the book of Revelation.

"God works in a mysterious way His wonders to perform", says William Cowper, the poet and hymn-writer: on that Park the Gospel of Christ was also shared with a lady who mentioned a relation in Guelph, Ontario, Canada. This relation sent her a Scripture Calendar at Christmas, and years later Ann and I were to stay with her on a later preaching tour in Canada! It is exciting being a Christian: you don't know what God is going to do next – that is when you go forward in faith in obedience to the Lord. Rev. Andrew MacBeath, my old Principal at the Glasgow B.T.I., used to say, *"God loves to surprise His children"*. How true!

This was hardly a very good start. However, just down the road a little bit was the Knocknagoney Hall, where I have been able to minister the Word and report on the work of the MMH over many years.

My 3rd Preaching and Deputation Visit To Belfast
25th – 29th October 1971

It was a time of trial, when the "Troubles" were at their height. On 18th October I phoned the Secretary of Wilton Square City Mission, this being a few days before leaving for Belfast, and there had been a number of bombs going off. "Yes, the meeting is on", I was told. "Yes", I replied – I would, D.V., be at the meeting as arranged, and would be staying with Tom Meaney. Ann was anxious whether it would be wise for me to go, and her family with their Ulster connections were unsure.

After a sleepless night, the Lord spoke to me on the morning of Tuesday 19th through *Proverbs 3:26*: "For the LORD shall be thy confidence, and shall keep thy foot from being taken." (from *Daily Light*). This promise from God's Word gave me peace, settled my heart, and gave me the assurance that the Lord would undertake and provide. The heading for October 25th was *Psalm 71:16*, "I will go in the strength of the Lord GOD."

My concern was not in going to Belfast, but in crossing the City from East to Centre. On the night of October 26^{th,} they sent a taxi for me, and we passed an Army roadblock, i.e. checkpoint, as we travelled to Wilton Square City Mission. On arrival at the long, narrow hall (later blown up), it was filled with people. The Lord was with us, and on the stroke of 9 p.m. a taxi arrived and took me back in the dark to Lichfield Avenue where the vigilantes were active and stopped the taxi. I explained that my box was an Aldis Projector box that had been used for a Christian meeting, and that I was staying with Tom Meaney at No. 31. At this crucial moment, thankfully Tom arrived on the scene to support me amidst the excited crowd, and we walked back to his home for supper with his wife Irene. So, the Lord protected me, as promised. Praise His wonderful name!

On the overnight ferry from Liverpool to Belfast for this visit, a young commercial traveller shared a cabin with me. He listened to my testimony of God's saving grace and gladly received a "Good News for Modern Man" Gospel of St. John. He was encouraged to get right with God.

Preaching the Gospel… In Northern Ireland
(From the contemporaneous records of Mission Director Hector Hall.)

On the way to **Strangford Caravan Park** a Roman Catholic kindly gave me a lift part of the way. I explained that Christ was the only way to God, and gave him a tract.

A Presbyterian – an electronics engineer – gave me a lift to Downpatrick and asked me what I thought about eternal punishment in Hell (he had been discussing it with fellows at work). "Jesus spoke more about Hell than any other person in the New Testament. God does not will that any should perish but that all should come to repentance", I replied. He also asked, "What did our Lord mean by 'many mansions'?" I replied that He has gone to Heaven to prepare a place for His believing people; therefore 'many mansions' speaks of the Lord's provision for His people. We all too quickly reached the road junction where we had to part. He was very interested and sorry to say Good-bye. "You have a nice way of expressing things", he said as he thanked me for a Gospel in modern English.

The residential Caravan Park – though listed in the Caravan Sites Handbook – had not yet been developed, so I gave out the "*Emergency Post*" to people at the scattered cottages along the road back to Downpatrick. One lady – doing gardening – said she had bought Billy Graham's book '*Peace with God*' from a Bangor colporteur. I quoted *Romans 5:1*: "Being justified by faith, we have peace with God through our Lord Jesus Christ". I left her to think over this truth, as prayer ascended to the throne of grace.

I revisited **Knocknagoney Caravan Park**, Belfast and met Mr. B. for the first time. He invited me in and we discussed the false teaching of a heretical group who were resident on the Park. I asked him if he was born again. He replied, "No". "Would you *like* to be born again? Jesus said you must be born again, if you are to enter the Kingdom of God." He was unable to answer in the affirmative. He lost his wife recently and knew that life is short and that judgement is certain. Please pray for this man's salvation. He is near the Kingdom. A young unsaved man – brought up in a Gospel Hall – showed interest and gave me an invitation to pay a return visit, as it was time for me to leave the park.

At **Groomsport Caravan Park** near Bangor a gang of painters were re-decorating the toilets and other outbuildings as it was the end of the holiday season, and individually they were urged to give their hearts and lives to Christ. The manager invited me into his office, and when I asked him if he knew the Lord Jesus as his personal Saviour, he burst out laughing! He was given Christian literature, and we discussed the sites generally in Northern Ireland. He told me he had been to Rev. Ian Paisley's church, but he couldn't get a seat.

At **Helens Bay Caravan Park**, a Christian lady – the owner's wife – gave me permission to visit the people at any time. Two girls from Leeds briefly listened to the Gospel, as the rain came down.

Other Encouraging Meetings were held; on Wednesday 27th October at Bloomfield Baptist Church – the Church where Mrs. Ann Hall had heard the Gospel of Christ, and was converted when in her teens through the ministry of Pastor Willie Mullan – I showed a Coloured Slides presentation of the work of the Lord through the MMH.

Thursday 28th at 2.30 p.m. at the Iron Hall Assembly – Women's Meeting.

Thursday 28th at 8 p.m. at Knocknagoney Hall – a Coloured Slides presentation.

There isn't space to give details of the meetings, except to report that they were generally well attended and spiritually alive. Real interest was shown in this evangelistic ministry and the fellowship was warm-hearted and generous. I also thank Tom and Irene Meaney for their fellowship and gracious hospitality. Please remember the political situation in your prayers. Praise the Lord, and pray to the Lord to send forth a Northern Ireland representative for the MMH.

On the ferry home a medical student at Queens University discussed Christ's claims. He found it difficult to accept that Christ was the only way to God (*John 14:6*). He was challenged to read John's account of the life of Christ and to ask God to speak to him. Please pray for this young man's conversion.

During the "Troubles, I noticed that soldiers were gathered outside the Grove Baptist Church in East Belfast. I don't know why they were stationed there, but on the Poster Board outside the Church building were words from *Job 22:21*:

"ACQUAINT NOW THYSELF WITH GOD,
AND BE AT PEACE."

---

28   The Gospel, an Umbrella and a Dog?

There are two Mobile home Parks in St. Brides Wentlooge, south of **Newport**, Gwent, in South Wales. The main, larger one, with the striking name Lighthouse Park, is situated down by the Bristol Channel, and the other one is The Church House Inn Park, in the centre of the village.

My visit to this park will be always etched in my memory. When I first went there, there were just half-a-dozen single unit Mobile Homes at the rear of this small field. (On my last sight of this park it had a high brick wall and gates with 'Lions' on either side on the top of the wall, and with modern bungalow-type mobile homes: quite a contrast.) On this visit on 24th May 1973, it was just a field, with residential mobile homes along the bottom side. I prayed for God's blessing and guidance, and then called at each home to tell them of **Christ the Saviour**, starting from the left-hand side.

"God has not been very good to me," said a lady who backslidden spiritually. I answered by saying that God loved her so much that He sent His Son to die on the Cross of Calvary to redeem her at great cost. "If you have problems take them to the Lord in prayer. He will help you."

At another home a lady said that trusting in Jesus had helped her friend. She went on to say, "I am living on borrowed time. I had a heart attack six months ago... I would like to make my peace with God before I depart this life." I showed her *Romans 5:1*: "Being justified by faith, we have peace with God through our Lord Jesus Christ." I also shared *Romans 3:23* and *6:23* from my New Testament, and told her not to leave it too late, but to call upon the name of the Lord and be saved, today.

As I walked from one mobile home to another, two dogs, one large and one small, started to follow-me. However, I continued the ministry as before. At the next home I met a man – a son of the Manse – who said that, "he didn't believe in God", "it is all tripe!" He used the usual arguments of rationalists, but the Holy Spirit gave me answers to his questions. God in His wisdom knows best. He was challenged: "YOU must repent of your sins and get right with God, or you will have to give an account to God on the Day of Judgement," I said.

On finishing the Gospel Outreach I started to walk back slowly across the field. The two dogs followed me; the larger one was a rough-looking mongrel, and unknown to me, came silently up from behind and suddenly bit me on my right leg.   As I came away from the Park – at that very moment – I met a man and a woman. I was about to give them each a tract when I felt blood trickling down my right leg, and suddenly realised what had happened. The lady quickly and kindly said, "My brother lives above the Post Office and he will take you in his car to The Royal Gwent Hospital, in Newport." Which he kindly did. How thankful to God I was for this unexpected help. How good God *is* in arranging such help (*Romans 8:28*).

Why did this dog attack me? That morning before leaving the home of Ian and Judy Walker, Ian had kindly suggested that I take their umbrella, as rain was forecast. Had the dog been hit by an umbrella in the past? Quite possibly! Dogs might not have as good long-term memories as Elephants, but they do remember... On the spiritual level, there is a battle going on for the souls of men and women. Satan (see *Ephesians 6:12*) does not like his captives hearing of the true freedom and deliverance that Christ brings to repentant sinners.

Thus I arrived at **The Royal Gwent Hospital** – Accident and Emergency Unit. The Clerk of Admissions asked, "What do you do for a living?" "I am an evangelist – a preacher of the Gospel of Christ." "What is your date of birth?" (24th May 1937.) It happened to be my birthday! They soon had me in the Operating Theatre, put four stitches in my right leg, gave me a Tetanus Toxoid injection, and I was soon on my way. A good job efficiently done.

Providentially, across the road from the hospital was the Bus Stop for Cardiff, and so I was able to travel on to Porthkerry Residential Caravan Park to follow-up previous contacts. I then returned to Cardiff for the evening meeting in the home of our good friends Colin and Dulcie Wilks, and friends came from Heath Evangelical Church (Minister the Rev. Vernon Higham, a gifted preacher and hymn-writer). An up-to-date report of *Evangelism Among Mobile Home People* was given: in the meeting were two Doctors, if more medical help had been needed! Personal evangelism was encouraged and prayer for the MMH, and Christ was honoured. It taught me the Lord is in control - see *Romans 8:28*.

It was good, of course, to renew fellowship with Colin, and Dulcie and her Mum, with thanks for their hospitality.

The following are some further notes that I recorded of God's blessing on that memorable 5th Evangelistic and Deputation visit to South Wales.

A Backslider Restored to Blessing.

In late May 1974 I was asked by a teacher at Emmanuel Grammar School, Swansea – a school attached to the Bible College of Wales – to call and see a young married woman with a young child, who had married a Roman Catholic and whose marriage had sadly broken up. After prayer, the visit was made and I was invited into her home where I had the opportunity to listen to her story. I then felt God leading me to read the prophet *Joel Ch 2* and give her *verses 25-26* as a promise to be claimed:

> *Joel 2:25-26* "And I will <u>restore</u> to you the years that the locust hath eaten, the cankerworm, and the caterpiller, and the palmerworm... and ye shall eat in plenty, and be satisfied, and PRAISE the name of the LORD your God."

I prayed with her that the Lord would help her to repent of her sins and return to the Lord. The Holy Spirit was at work. She wrote to me two weeks later:

> *Porthkerry Caravan Park*
> *Rhoose, South Wales*
> *(Postmark – 12th June 1974)*

Dear Mr. Hall,

I hope you are well and family.

I have decided to begin reading the Bible again, that the Lord will meet me. I've never doubted that Jesus is alive but I've been a fool – I let the world and its things crowd in and on my life and never stopped to think of anything else. I know they are worthless but still attract me; stupid isn't it?

But the name of JESUS has an attraction still. He must meet me because I must know Him for myself. Please pray that He will meet with me.

> *Yours sincerely,*

> *Mrs. R. __*

Praise God! the Lord did meet with her in a real way in grace and mercy, and she started attending a local Elim Church. A year later she had – after prayer – been led of God to start a Children's Meeting in her Mobile Home at 3pm on Sundays.

She then wrote:

"I expect you will be wondering how we are getting on and if we got

a Sunday School going. This is about the 4ᵗʰ week; the kids seem to love it!! The first week we had only one little boy which was a bit disappointing but since then it has caught on with the kids and they have been attracting each other. We have a regular group of 7 and some others have asked to come next week. I'm not an organising genius but I left it with the Lord and He has drawn them.

We have been learning about the 'World God Made'. To give illustrations we have been sticking cut-out stars and many clouds etc. in books – the kids have their own which they can take home once full, and of course we learn a Bible verse to go with the cut-outs. The kids really love it.

So please Pray for us. I'm sure the Lord will bless us. Two of the little girls had never heard of Jesus, and didn't know Who He was and it was such a unique experience to begin to tell them.

Now will you tell me the vision the Lord gave you concerning the Caravan Parks. Anything He said about them interests me, I suppose because I live in one."

29   Adrian Underwood
MMH Leicestershire Evangelist

Adrian Underwood had been an agricultural engineer before studying at the Bible Training Institute, Glasgow – the same college as the author.

Adrian's Conversion

In the Application Form to join the Mission to Mobile Homes, question No 10 asked, "When were you converted to God, and under what circumstances?"

Adrian wrote: *"Converted June 20ᵗʰ '65, through the singing of the hymn 'Rock of Ages'. In the May of '65 the Lord convicted me of the need of Salvation through the ministry of Mr. M. Keen, then a NYLC evangelist".* In giving a character reference Rev. Geoffrey Grogan, the then Principal of BTI, wrote of Adrian: "He has a great love for people, and an intense desire to bring them to CHRIST."

Adrian had a very good Commissioning Service at Melbourne Hall Evangelical Free Church, Leicester, with over one hundred people present. The Lord's presence was very evident. The Young People sang, "SO SEND I YOU to suffer for My sake" and Adrian told how the Lord had led him into the work of the Mission. His pastor Dr. Eric Gurr then led in prayer, setting our brother apart for the Lord's work; and I gave a closing Message from *2 Timothy 4:1* and told of WHAT GOD is DOING among the mobile home park people. Also encouraging them to faithfully pray for Adrian in the coming days as he would be tested and tried.

Although Adrian served for less than two years with the Mission, he did valuable outreach work in personally taking the Gospel of Christ to people on the mobile home parks in and around Leicester. These were early days in the work of the MMH, and looking back with the perspective of almost forty years, Adrian was the first full-time evangelist – apart from myself – working with the Mission, just six years after its inception.

The MMH was still 'finding its feet' at this time, so it was a significant STEP of FAITH to appoint another full-time worker. Council Members gave much thought and prayer to this appointment.

Letter Sent Out to Prayer Partners

In the letter sent out on 8th November 1973 to our MMH Prayer Partners regarding ADRIAN'S appointment I wrote:

"Do remember our brother in your prayers, that the Lord will give him all needed grace. This is a BIG STEP of FAITH for him and also for the Mission, but we are CONFIDENT that OUR FAITHFUL GOD WILL MEET ALL our NEEDS 'according to HIS RICHES in GLORY by CHRIST JESUS' Philippians 4:19."

Adrian stayed with our good friends Derek and Brenda Alcock of Reynard Way Evangelical Church during his probationary training period, and there he met a certain young lady by the name of Valerie, his future wife-to-be. So God guides in wonderful ways unknown to us. Adrian spoke at Moulton Evangelical Church, and was a 'cheerful chappie'! As Rev. Bryan Gilbert of *"One Step Forward"* wrote of Adrian in another reference, "He has a very cheerful disposition"! One particular light moment comes to mind: he was playing in our garden with Carolyn (then aged about seven) and Sharon (then about five), happily dancing around the lawn with them singing the popular song at that time: *"Wombles of Wimbledon Common"* – with obvious great delight – before tea and the mid-week meeting at Moulton Evangelical Church.

But, as you will see from the following reports, there was nothing superficial about him.

The following reports: **A)** "God's Guidance and Call" and **B)**

"Outreach in Leicestershire" appeared in the MMH '*Faith & Victory*' Newsletter at the time, and **C)** – Adrian's Report – is his full and complete report of his first year of evangelistic ministry on the Mobile Home Parks of Leicestershire.

If my memory serves me rightly, and I am confident that it does, Adrian received the gift of a good working car to do his gospel work; the Lord in His Faithfulness thus provides for His servants. Praise God!

A) God's Guidance and Call to The Mission

"For some years I have received the Magazine of the Mission to Mobile Homes. Although being aware of the need for an evangelist, and praying that the need would be supplied, I had no idea that I would be the one of God's choice.

Being an associate member of the FEBV (Fellowship for Evangelising Britain's Villages) means that one can share in the fellowship prayer letter. Whilst reading the FEBV prayer letter, the Director of the Mission to Mobile Homes, Mr. H. Hall, noted that I was seeking the Lord's guidance for my future service. Mr. Hall then wrote to me in relation to the need of the Mission. At this time, I was in pursuit of the possibility of another sphere of service, and therefore thought service with the Mission improbable. However, the Lord taught me to labour for the things which do not perish (John 6:27). This, and the closing of other doors, was to show me that my service was to be with the Mission, and to work with Mr. Hall.

Many people have expressed their willingness to share in prayer fellowship. This was wonderfully manifest at the commissioning service at Melbourne Hall on 14th November. There was a real sense of the presence of the Lord. I thank Dr. Gurr, the Elders, and the fellowship at Melbourne Hall, for their fellowship in the work of the Lord.

A.D. Underwood."

B) Outreach in Leicestershire. *By A. Underwood.*

*"Praise God for the good reception on **Countesthorpe Caravan Park**. There are a number of open homes for the Gospel. May it be that on subsequent visits I might have greater opportunity to speak of the Lord and the need of the soul's salvation.*

*On **Littlethorpe Caravan Park** I met Mrs. H. who is very lonely. By her own confession she is a Christian. Her husband, also a Christian, was in hospital. I was able to bring a little comfort to her in the reading* *of the scripture and prayer and later I visited her husband in Leicester General Hospital.*

Praise God for the Churches (Baptist) in these villages. The ministry is a ministry of the Lord with the power of the Holy Spirit. It gives one confidence in the work to know there are people of God at hand.

I was invited in to meet an elderly lady who was a spiritualist, at **Linkfield Road Caravan Park**. *She spoke of the transfiguration and the resurrection, as she believed them to be. Her son, J., did not subscribe to the 'doctrine' of his mother, but had his own thoughts concerning the scriptures. He was very mixed up. I had to point out that the flight of Lot from Sodom, and the escape of Peter from prison were not one-in-the-same story. Almost all of his knowledge of the Bible came from films with Bible stories for their base.*

'I can give you ten minutes' came the reply from Mr. M. at **'The Green' Caravan Park** *and for that ten minutes we spoke of man's Sin in relation to the Holy God. He said 'I want to be clean, to start life all over again'. His past life was in a mess, he wanted to be rid of it and start again. May the SGM booklet 'A New Start' be used by the Holy Spirit to bring about a Godly conviction of Sin and repentance of heart leading to eternal life.*

C) Adrian's Report
(a) People 'Helped' Through My Ministry
It is difficult to say how many people have been 'helped' through the past year. When I think of J.L. and A.M. I am assured I have been of little help. These people are still far from the Lord, with not a thought of repentance and faith toward God. I think of a lady at Stony Stratford who made an attempt on her life. She willingly accepted a John's Gospel and said she would read it. On my next visit she had moved away: we can only pray the Word of the Lord would work in her heart. There was a lady at Princethorpe who always looked forward to my visit. She was kind and often gave me a kind word. She was very friendly and willing to speak of the Lord Jesus Christ. Another lady on the site is a cripple but she is always left with something to read. When I call she is at work but again we pray for the light of the Word to be upon her.

There are others like a Salvationist at Ellistown who is happy there is someone witnessing on the parks of our land. A Jewish person had little time to speak of the Lord Jesus. Three ladies who asked me what I was selling were surprised at the answer, "Giving something!" They listened to the message of the Saviour and each took a tract. A lady who said she was an Agnostic took tracts and said she would read them. One J.W. lady was willing to talk for a short time, also a man in his garden accepted tracts and a short witness. The R.C. lady at Mountsorrel always has a smile for me and receives the Emergency Post. Mrs. H. of Littlethorpe is always thankful for a visit. I must never leave out the Lord's Prayer in our Bible reading and prayer time together, Mrs. Hancock of Buxton was thankful for fellowship in the Lord. She is a Christian and worships at the local Methodist Church. News has reached me of a lady who expressed to a friend how thankful she is that there is someone with an interest in her. This lady has been visited a number of times. Both her and her husband are very open to the Gospel. She has a son who is a missionary in Brazil with UFM, and on occasions visits an evangelical church in Coventry.

(b) The Spiritual Need of the People on the Sites.
This is as follows: -
> *People living in darkness, needing illumination.*
> *People living in sin, needing salvation.*
> *People living unholy lives, needing sanctification.*

The above seems to sum up the need of the people in this land who live on Mobile Home Parks. But there is also a need for them to feel real, true, warm friendship. Many, many people are lonely, and are in need of someone to call on them and listen to their problems. This, in turn, gives great opportunity to bring the message of the Lord Jesus Christ. I have found the greatest problem is winning the friendship of my 'flock'. It has been proved to me that the greater friendship I can show, the easier is the opportunity to speak of Christ. On the parks where I am known there is good relations and freedom to witness to the saving grace of the Lord.

(c). The importance of the use of good literature *in the work cannot be over emphasized. This is a vital link with the people on the sites. During the absence of the evangelist, the printed word can still be working. The booklet 'Words of Comfort' (SGM) has been of blessing to a number of people. This is the most used book when working with old people. One occasion, the book was given to a lady who had recently lost her husband. The scripture readings were of great comfort to her, and she told her sister about her 'little book'. Upon reading, the sister asked if she too could have one. This book in now in her hands and we pray the Lord to bless it. Giving good literature and backing the same with prayer will bring forth to word of the Lord with great power.*

(d) Tracts Used.

During a six-month period, the approximate numbers of tracts used were:

Emergency Post	*700-800.*
Victory T.C.	*200 plus.*
S.G.M.	*100 plus.*

30   First MMH House Parties...
...at "Alveston Leys" 9th – 11th May 1975

When we were living in Northampton I ventured once a month to Birmingham for the Birmingham Missionary Prayer Fellowship, held in the bungalow home of Edrie Mallard's mother, in Kings Heath. It was a real means of grace to me, and the friends were most welcoming, with a real concern for the worldwide spread of the Gospel of Christ. The Chairman was the Rev. Tom Simpson (S.I.M. – Sudan Interior Mission) and the Secretary was Miss Margaret Brown.   They arranged a Missionary Conference from time to time in King's Heath Evangelical Church and graciously included me in this to report on the work of the MMH. Pastor Paul Mallard later became a Council of Reference member of the MMH and preached at a number of meetings for us, which was appreciated.

I happened to ask Margaret Brown if she knew of any suitable Centre for a Mission House Party. She immediately mentioned "Alveston Leys", which was part of the Church of England Children's Society. It catered for small conferences and was situated in Alveston Village, just a few miles south of Stratford-Upon-Avon, a town made famous by a certain play-wright – guess who? Alveston Leys had the most beautiful English Garden, and its accommodation suited us down to a peach. There were lovely views from most of the bedrooms and the food was excellent.

The Theme: 'Workers Together With Jesus'
Speakers Expected:
Evangelists: REG TOMLINSON, Evesham.
HECTOR HALL, MMH Director
and MMH Council Members

We arrived on the Friday afternoon, so as to settle in, to see that everything was in order, and to be ready to welcome guests. After an excellent meal prepared by our hosts, Mr. and Mrs. Heeley, we gathered for a Welcome and Prayer Meeting for God's blessing on the weekend.

Then Ann and I, together with our daughters Carolyn and Sharon, took an evening stroll in Alveston Village – it being dark by then. We walked along by a stream – and almost walked onto a Swan's nest situated on the path (this fact we didn't realise till the next day!).

The MMH Council met briefly on the Saturday morning, under the Chairmanship of Mr. Peter Assheton. We all enjoyed fellowship over an excellent Lunch, and then spent a relaxing afternoon in Stratford-Upon-Avon, visiting Shakespeare's birth place, and enjoying the River Avon.

On our return to Alveston Leys, the Director gave an up-to-date Coloured Slides presentation of the expanding Gospel Outreach of The Mission to Mobile Homes. I had written to our brother Reg Tomlinson on 7th May, '*It would be nice if you and Grace could come for a meal at 7 pm and then the meeting at 8 pm. It will be a small House Party, but we are looking to the Lord to richly bless His word and use it for His glory.*'

A brief report, written later, records; 'It was a joy to come apart and rest awhile in May in the Lord's presence, to refresh the spirit, to renew one's vision of the Lord, to clarify one's vision of the Lord's will for the Mission, to renew fellowship with the Lord's people, and to make new friends.'

We much enjoyed Reg Tomlinson's message on Saturday evening, on '*How to be a Fruitful Christian*', based on *John Chapter 15.*
John 15:5 'I am the Vine, ye are the branches: He that abideth in Me, and I in Him, the same bringeth forth much fruit: for without Me ye can do NOTHING."

In his younger days Reg had worked as a horticulturist, cultivating and maintaining garden plants, so his message concerning our union with Christ was most helpful. Abiding in Christ – necessary pruning bringing forth more growth – and letting Christ's word abide in us, brings forth fruit for **His** glory.

A Sad Memory
Reg Tomlinson was later to be called as Pastor of an Evangelical Church in Bassano, Alberta, Canada. One day Ann and I were visiting friends, and after tea they put on the 6 o'clock News on the BBC, when there was a "News Flash", to say that an English Pastor and his wife had been shot dead in Alberta. You have no doubt guessed – it was Reg and Grace. It appears that they had led a woman in the Church to Saving Faith in Christ: the husband strongly objected and shot Reg and Grace. We

know that sudden death is sudden glory for the Christian. Grace was a gifted singer, so she will – with Reg – be singing in the Choir of Heaven.

"Worthy is the Lamb that was slain."

There was one consolation; that they had no children, but they were of course dearly missed by other family members and by the Lord's people, including the many children they had led to Christ.

The Apostle Paul sums it up:

Philippians 1:21 For me to live is **Christ**, and to die is **gain**.

A Happy Memory of Reg and Grace Tomlinson

At this point I would like to pay a few words of tribute to Reg and Grace. A short while after coming to Lincolnshire Ann and I, with our young girls Carolyn and Sharon, were on holiday at Anderby Creek, staying in a kind friend's caravan. We were out on the beach one day enjoying ourselves when Reg and Grace appeared with their team of Christians, wearing their bright orange shirts and blouses and singing heartily:

Sunshine Corner is here again,
With the Gospel clear and plain,
Never mind the weather
Let's all get together,
Sunshine Corner is here again!

Children and adults would gather around them, when they would sing a chorus or two, read the Scriptures from which a memory verse was taught, and be given a bible message. After the Sunday afternoon Gospel Meeting in the Methodist chapel at Chapel St. Leonards, they invited us as a family to go back with them to the house where the team was based for tea and a time of fellowship, which we enjoyed.

Reg and Grace worked with the National Young Life Campaign (N.Y.L.C.). Frederick B. Wood of the N.Y.L.C. wrote books that I avidly read as a young Christian in my teens. *'Christian Certainty'* was one such book, with such clarity with regard to the Gospel of Christ and the way of salvation, for which I truly thank God.

Second Alveston Leys House Party 7th – 9th May 1976.

It was the best yet! As guests arrived they found the house decorated with a variety of beautiful flowers (left from the local Flower Festival). After a good evening meal, prepared by Mr. and Mrs. Heeley and staff, we met in the lounge where Peter Assheton, our Acting Chairman, showed us most interesting coloured slides of his recent visit to the Holy Land. Our Saturday Morning Prayer Session in the Chapel, based on *Acts 12*, was a time of believing prayer. At the morning Conference Session, the Rev. George Ely of Oxford expounded *Psalm 34* for our spiritual enrichment. We had a beautiful afternoon for the outing to Hagley Hall, where we had tea under the tree, as it was so hot – a great afternoon for the children!

Evangelist William Davie spoke on '**God the Great Provider**' at the evening Conference Session, and outlined some of the problems encountered on the West of Scotland Mobile Home sites. The Sunday morning Prayer Session, led by Mr. Nigel Barber (Council Member), reminded us that we are engaged in a battle with the enemy (*Ephesians Chapter 6*). Prayer went up to the Throne of Grace for victory in the work of the Mission and in our home churches. In the Communion Service our brother Pastor Bernard Lambert preached movingly on '**Progressive Christian Experience Right up to the Gates of Heaven.**' Indeed, our Crucified King drew near to us, as we remembered Calvary. It was a fitting conclusion to a Conference weekend of much blessing!

31   Nivensknowe & Pentland Mission (Caravan Church)

How did the work at Loanhead come about, you may well ask?

At the Call of God, I visited the Mobile Home Parks across the central belt of Scotland in the summer of 1967, sharing the Gospel of Christ with all I met. On the 25th of July of that year I ventured forth to the Nivensknowe Park at Loanhead – but how did I know that these residential Parks existed? It was during my time with the Railway Mission that I had first noticed these two large Parks (Nivensknowe & Pentland) as I travelled in a No.70 Bus from St. Andrews Bus Station, Edinburgh, to Peebles to preach at the Peebles Railway Mission.

The Nivensknowe & Pentland Parks were the two largest Mobile Home Parks in Scotland, with 153 and 205 homes respectively. It wasn't surprising they were so large, since they offered almost instant accommodation to low wage earners, and were situated just south of the Scottish Capital. On arrival on the afternoon of 25th from my home in Beith, Ayrshire I asked Mr. Londi of the Nivensknowe Park for permission to visit the residents, and to encourage them to have faith in Christ. As his name suggests he was of Italian origin, and he was in the

89

near future to prove of considerable help to the MMH. He gave me permission and said, "You might do some good".

Through this initial visit a number of children were contacted, and when asked if they went to Sunday School or Bible Class only one had any such connection. There was obviously a need on the Park for a Sunday School. More importantly there were in God's providence some Christians on the Park, and His wider plan to include the Pentland Park next door was revealed.

Workers Together with Jesus *(2 Corinthians 6:1)*

I met Kath Brady and later her husband Alex, who worked at the nearby Bilston Glen Colliery, dealing with miners' health issues. He was a gifted singer and played the Accordion. They gave me tea and I enjoyed their fellowship in the Lord. Dr. Valerie Hey was an anaesthetist in the Western Hospital, and was also to be a great help, and one of the future teachers. Also, there was a Salvation Army lady and a Pentecostal lady who were believers. They all agreed there was a need for a Sunday school on the Park. They later convened a meeting and decided to start a Sunday school on the first Sunday in October, with classes in different homes, and with the approval of Mr. Londi. So, I returned home to Ann on that first visit to Nivensknowe Park with some excitement, and Praise to God for His blessing and the beginning of the unfolding of **His** plans for the work and witness at Loanhead.

Later, Mr. Ian and Mrs. Margaret Wright started a Sunday School on the Pentland Park in their own home for children on that park. They served very faithfully for a few years, teaching the children Bible stories, choruses and memory verses. Eventually, however, since they had a growing family they were offered a house and so moved away. It meant no Sunday School on the Pentland Park, although some of the children, but not many, regularly attended the Nivensknowe Sunday School.

When Dr. Hay took up a new medical appointment, in Manchester I think it was, the Nivensknowe Sunday School temporarily stopped. But in the will of the Lord I happened to be up in Scotland on deputation at the Park, and in visitation and follow-up met David and Anna Bowers. They had recently come from Belfast to live on the Park, and were keen to re-start the Sunday School in their home. Praise God! They served faithfully and acceptably for a couple of years.

(Later, in 1980, they went with their family to serve faithfully as Missionaries for quite a number of years with the Irish Baptist Foreign

Mission in PERU.)

As time went on and prayers ascended to the Throne of Heavenly Grace the Lord revealed what was needed was a large mobile home, converted (good word!) to seat 20 people with a lectern/pulpit and with a kitchen and toilet at the far end. Thus, there could be not only a Sunday School, but also a Sunday-night Gospel Meeting for adults, and mid-week meetings. After prayer, I contacted Mr. Londi to sound him out. He was – praise God – quite favourable, and said initially that it would cost £450, but later adjusted it to £300. That is equivalent to £1,800 in today's money, which of course we didn't have. The MMH Council had authorized the opening of a New Projects Fund, and prayer was made for God to supply this sum. Also, one anonymous person promised to give gifts toward its provision. It was also mentioned in *'Faith & Victory'*; the Lord answered prayer – and provided.

Rev. Andrew MacBeath's Letter
At the time of the Dedication of the Caravan Mission Church, we received the following kind letter from Rev. MacBeath, the Principal of the Bible Training Institute (B.T.I.), Glasgow.

29 Arisaig Drive, Bearsden, 13.5.71.

My dear Hector,

It is a great joy in these days of widespread apathy to hear of the seal God is setting on your Outreach to Mobile Homes.

Recently I have felt afresh that the love of Christ ought to warm our hearts so that no man or woman, however sordid their life, can be shrugged off or treated with coolness or disrespect. The precious blood of Christ avails for them too, and it is our business to tell and tell again our thrilling news of redemption and our indwelling Saviour Who creates within us a clean heart.

May the meeting at Loanhead on Saturday (Dedication of the Caravan Church Project) be one of thrill and triumph.

Heartily Yours,

(Signed) Andrew MacBeath

The report in 'Faith & Victory'

Psalm 127:1 "Except the LORD build the house they labour in vain that build it."

Dedication of Nivensknowe & Pentland Mission

The Caravan Mission Church at Loanhead, Midlothian, was dedicated to the glory of God by Mr. Hector Hall, director of The Mission to Mobile Homes, assisted by the Rev. Charles Gillaitry, on Saturday 15th May 1971.

Christian friends from Portobello Baptist Church and Duns Mission joined Loanhead friends in thanksgiving to God for the provision of this Caravan in His faithfulness. The £300 had all been prayed in, claiming the promises of God. A letter was read from the Rev. A. MacBeath, president of the Mission, who was unable to be present due to recuperation following an operation.

Children packed the caravan for the School on the Sunday afternoon taken by Mr. David Squibb. Mr. Squibb ably assisted Mr. Hall in visiting a large number of residents of both parks, commending Christ and inviting people to the opening services. The devil put all in our way, as the caravan had not been converted (!) or sited when we arrived. The Lord knew we were anxious, and on the Thursday evening He gave me the promise, 'They shall fight against thee; but they shall NOT PREVAIL AGAINST THEE; for I AM WITH THEE, saith the LORD, to DELIVER THEE.' Jeremiah 1:19

Amongst those attending the evening service were former Sunday School teachers: Dr. Valerie Hey (from Manchester) who presented a beautifully embroidered picture of a Cross and Anchor which she had made; Mr. & Mrs. Alex Brady, and Mrs. M. Wight. Mr. Brady sang two solos, Mr. Squibb testified and Mr. Hall brought God's message from Isaiah 61.

Sequel *- Mr. Alex Marshall has been assisting since the end of May. He tells me as many as 30 children attend the Sunday School some Sundays. They now have classes. A Junior Church has been started for the teenagers. Some are near to commitment to Christ. Numbers at the evening Gospel service are small but new people are attending. Please pray that souls may be saved, to serve the Lord within the fellowship.*

May Christ the Head of the Church, rule this Church, with Mr. Marshall and helpers working together with the Lord, 'To the Praise of His glory'.

Alex Marshall from Bathgate

(who became Lay Pastor of the Pentland Mission Church).

Alex and his wife Ann were committed Christians who had had the sad experience of losing a baby. I don't know all the circumstances: only someone who has had that experience can fully understand the trauma. It led to Alex's back-sliding (possibly blaming God for the loss?). I also don't know how long this was for, but the Lord is ever mindful of His children, and brought about the circumstances to bring healing to him and his wife.

On a flight to Belfast, Alex happened in the providence of God to sit in a seat next to Alex Campbell, a Christian businessman who had a handicapped child. (Alex Campbell was an elder at The Iron Hall Assembly, whom I later got to know quite well. A fine Christian man, who kindly took me out to lunch on a couple of occasions in difficult days.) Alex Campbell testified to the Goodness of God, to him, his wife and his child. This had the effect of causing Alex Marshall to decide to return to the Lord, and when I met him at Bethany Hall, Bathgate, he was very keen to serve the Lord, and to go with the Gospel to people on the mobile home parks in his area of Scotland. He became our MMH representative in the area, before serving at the 'Caravan Church'.

His Farewell Letter that follows gives a flavour of his faithful service in which his wife ably supported him. He faithfully sowed the seed of God's Word in many hearts, young and old. For three years he travelled from Bathgate to Loanhead each Lord's day and mid-week, in all weathers.

Alex Marshall's "Farewell Letter" – March 1974.

One day soon as the Sun sets behind the Pentland Hills, it will also be setting on my work in the Nivensknowe-Pentland Mission Church after a period of almost three years. What will there be to look back to?

Sunday after Sunday of pouring rain! Driving through ice and heavy snow, not knowing whether it would be possible to get back home!

Travelling over 9,000 miles as a total to take the services and often finding one or two adults for the evening service! Was it worth it all? Of course it was, because it was being done for the Glory of God who called and promised to be faithful to those who answer the call. The work has been hard and, on the surface, unrewarding, but God did not intend a work for Him to be easy, or at least Satan makes sure it is not.

*What has been achieved since this Church was opened? NOTHING... that is by the way of a large congregation or financial intake ... nothing that I have done during my period as pastor here that I can show you. However, GOD **has** been working in a wonderful way in this little Church which only seats 20 People: we pack quite a few more children in for the Sunday School.*

*Since May 1971 my wife and I have taught over 200 children THE LOVE OF JESUS at this Sunday School and Junior Church group, **God** really brought them in. Through some of those children God has taken the Gospel to places I could not go to. The first to go were two of the children... they went to AFRICA with their parents: these children like all our children love the Gospel Choruses, and I know that they used to sing them in their homes as well as at play. (They were Angela & Paula.)*

Then there was Jacqueline and her brother, who are of a travelling family, who have gone to GREECE: this young girl took some literature with her, which we gave as a present before she left.

Terresa went to BRUSSELS where her parents work; she always comes to the Sunday School when the parents come back to Scotland. Next time she comes she will be old enough to attend Junior Church.

Young Sandra has just recently gone to GERMANY where her father serves in the Air Force: she only attended Sunday School for a short period but soon picked up the choruses. Two travelling families who are back on the road will be singing such choruses as "Jesus' Love is very wonderful" and "Deep and Wide" as they travel along. So God will use the little ones to carry The Story wherever they go.

Adults from Manchester, London, Bristol, Cornwall, America, and the North, South, East and West of Scotland have attended services in this little Church which is often referred to as "Only an old second-hand Caravan" but the "Old, old Story" is the important one that is preached here.

No matter how heavy the rain or the snow you will be sure of a sea of young smiling faces waiting to greet you.

We pray that some day, some one will stand in testimony and say, 'I first heard the Gospel of Christ in a little Caravan Church in Loanhead'.

Signed: Alex Marshall, Pastor.

32 Pentland Mission Church – Continued Ministry

The last chapter concluded with the Farewell Letter from the first Lay Pastor, Alex Marshall.

*This chapter now tells of the continuance of the work, by **Ron and Mary Borthwick** in the interim, and then by **John Norrie** as the second Lay Pastor, together with his wife **Jean**.*

Ron and Mary Borthwick

When Alex Marshall finished his ministry at Pentland Mission Church in March 1974 prayer went up to God for the continuance of the work and witness. In answer to those prayers, Ron and Mary Borthwick kindly offered to help in the short term, and thus I met them at Loanhead on the occasion of the 3rd Anniversary Meeting of the Mission Church, at which I was the guest preacher. John later wrote:

Edinburgh 14th May 1974.

Dear Hector,

It was very pleasant to meet you on Sunday morning (at the Caravan Church) and I just want to confirm that both Mary & I are willing to help in continuing the services in the interim.

It certainly would be worthwhile if a regular Evangelical ministry were maintained on the site.

Mary and I have never made it our practice to plan too far ahead as the Lord is our guide and Shepherd. If sheep go before the Shepherd they'll soon get lost! ...We are available to the Lord and ready to help in His work wherever He chooses.

We look forward to meeting Adrian [Underwood, MMH Leicester evangelist] – he will be able to weigh up the situation and God will guide him. We trust you are rested and refreshed after your hectic travels.

Yours sincerely,

Ron & Mary Borthwick.

Ron later wrote on 7th July 1974:

Thank you for your letter of the 7th of last month. We have just returned from a two-week holiday up in Lewis. ...My position is just the same as mentioned in my letter of 14th May... We have been keeping a regular note of offerings and the Sunday School has been well attended. There were 17 youngsters out today but no one at the Junior Church. This is of course a holiday fortnight.

As the weather was lovely we held our <u>Evening Service outside the Caravan</u> and one or two people stopped to hear the singing and the Word. "It has pleased God by the foolishness of preaching..." (1 Corinthians 1:21)

No doubt Adrian has reported on his 3 weeks here. It is a needy place. We trust you had a good holiday and God's peace reigns within.

Yours sincerely, Ronald G. Borthwick.

John Norrie

The second person that God called to serve as Lay Pastor at the MMH Caravan Mission Church at Pentland Mobile Home Park was Mr. John Norrie. John's period of service lasted less than two years, but they appear to have been fruitful years, particularly among the young people at the Mission, for which we give praise to God.

Here is Rev. Charles Gellaitry's report of his interview with John for the MMH Council; and John's personal Christian testimony.

Rev Charles Gellaitry, Minister of Portobello Baptist Church, our very helpful Council of Reference member for Edinburgh, in interviewing Mr. John Norrie concerning the Lay Pastorate, wrote on 17th April,1975:

Some little while ago he (i.e. John) was put in contact with Mr. & Mrs. Ronald Borthwick, who have been serving with the Caravan Church but were in a position that prohibited their continuing with their work there.

Mr. Norrie has been conducting the services at the Caravan Church for about the past five weeks – Sunday School, Junior Church and evening Gospel Service: in addition, he has been carrying out systematic tract work at both sites on each Friday evening.

Mr. Norrie worships in the Free Baptist Church in Penicuik, but has felt the Lord's leading to serving at the Caravan Church and seems happy to be committed to such a work for the Lord. He is married with one son. His wife is in complete agreement with his interest and concern for this ministry.

I had a good witness in my spirit of Mr. Norrie and I believe that, provided he satisfies all the requirements of the Council, he would be a desirable worker for the Mission. He affirms that he is in complete

96

agreement with the doctrinal basis of the Mission.

John Norrie's Testimony
(Given at the time of applying to the Mission.)

"I was converted 17 years ago. At that time I had just returned from America and Canada on tour with the PIPES and DRUMS of the BLACK WATCH, being a piper with the Regiment. I had tasted every imaginable pleasure of the world on the tour, but the conclusion was that my life was empty, without purpose. But GOD broke into my life on returning to Scotland.

I was now stationed at Redford Barracks, and it was there I heard the Gospel. An Army Scripture Reader came round the barracks telling us of Christ and salvation, and handing out Gospel tracts, God also spoke to me through a Christian piper. He had a peace and joy I didn't have, and it showed in his life. One Sunday this Christian asked me to go to a Gospel Rally in Edinburgh where I heard the message of salvation. I was convicted of sin during the meeting and recognised my need of Christ. The Scripture Reader's home wasn't far away, so he invited me to his home, and led me to the LORD there.

My life was transformed. I had the presence of Christ and a purpose for living, joy and peace flooded my soul. Since then the Lord has guided me and my family, sometimes through difficulties but He's been my strength. Now the Lord has led us into the Mission to Mobile Homes and we pray that He may use us for His glory."

John's Report at MMH Annual Meeting
Mr. John Norrie gave his report at the 7th Annual Meeting of "The Mission to Mobile Homes' held in the Manfield Hall, Moulton, Northampton, on Saturday 11th October 1975. He told of the increased numbers attending the Sunday School and Junior Church, but more support was needed for the adult meetings in the Pentland Mission Church.

Tokens of The Lord's Faithfulness
John wrote:

My own son, Ian, came to know the Lord last year in the Mission, and has gone on well since.

A number of young people have come to the Lord in this past year but find it difficult because of their home background.

John Norrie's Resignation

When John resigned as Lay Pastor on 12th December 1976, this was mainly due to the lack of support by adults on the Parks. The Mission appreciated all that he was able to do. He did see God's blessing as his son Ian came to know the Lord, and possibly other young lives were also thus transformed.

It does need to be taken in to consideration that the work in such residential Mobile Home Parks is especially difficult, as the movement of people is far greater than in traditional housing. Whilst a good number of people stay resident for many years, quite a number do move on to more traditional housing after a year or two, due to a growing family needing more accommodation, or to job opportunities further afield. This makes it doubly hard to build up a regular supporting congregation.

We thank John and his wife Jean for all their faithful service and ministry. We are sorry it didn't last longer; but only eternity will fully reveal all that was accomplished.

33   Pentland Mission Church – a New Chapter

*We here firstly introduce **Alex and Heather Higgins**, who were interim leaders of the Sunday School work at the Mission Church. Then follows the appointment of **James Brownlee** to the Pastorate, and some details of the Lord's work through that Pastorate.*

Much of this chapter is from contemporary letters and reports from that period.

Alex and Heather Higgins

After John Norrie resigned as Lay Pastor on 12th of December 1976, Mrs. Heather Higgins very kindly offered to carry on the Sunday School until a new pastor was appointed. The attendance reported was very good*. She and her husband Alex carried on faithfully until early the Summer of 1977. The Mission supplied them with Scripture Union Sunday School materials.

They wrote:

14th March 1977

Mr. Angus is always present, and a lady staying in Pentland temporarily brings her two children and sits in with my class, so I am pleased to have her help.

We will be interested to hear when a new pastor is appointed, and thank you and the Mission for your prayers for the Sunday School.

With warmest Christian greetings,

(Signed) Alex & Heather Higgins.

*On Some Sundays as many as twenty-four children attended, split into two classes. Heather taught the younger ones, and Alex the older ones.

James Brownlee's Call
James recorded his call to the work thus:

"Having taken a Service in the Mobile Homes Mission Church at Loanhead, Midlothian, I got a great burden for the work among the mobile home dwellers.

I tried to put it out of my mind, but the Lord laid it very forcibly on my heart.

Then when a Christian friend of mine who took some of the Services at the Mission Church, asked me about taking over the work at Loanhead, it confirmed it.

My motive is to see the Lord's name glorified, and to labour for Him in the extension of His Kingdom."

James Brownlee's Testimony
(In applying to the Mission)

"I was converted to Christ in the Salvation Army Hall, Henry Street, Enniskillen, Northern Ireland in May 1954. Since then I am sure there are many times when I failed the Lord, but I know HE has never once failed me. I can say of a surety all that I am, all that I have and all that I ever hope to be, I owe all to the keeping and saving power of the Lord Jesus Christ.

I at present worship with the Edinburgh City Mission (The Inch, Edinburgh).

I was a Sunday School Superintendent for three years. I also taught for a period, and I have currently taken part in visitation in the Inch Housing Scheme."

Finally, he says:
"I have endeavoured to lead others to Christ by personal witness, by testifying and preaching the Word."

Mr. Brownlee, even before he was inducted, showed his loving concern for people on the M.H. Parks in this:

Fire Tragedy at Loanhead

James Brownlee wrote to me in May 1977:

There was a fire disaster on the Caravan Park yesterday: the Caravan occupied by the Bennet family was completely destroyed and one boy who was disabled died in the fire.

I went out yesterday afternoon to visit the family. Mr. Bennet and the other boy is staying with his brother on the site at the moment. Mrs. Bennet is in hospital with severe burns to her hands.

I would value your prayers for this family, and for myself as I seek to visit them again, that I may be given the right words to speak to them at this time. Incidentally, the Bennet boy (Leslie?) who survived the fire came to the Sunday School for the first time last Sunday.

There are twenty-four children on the Sunday School roll, and sixteen families are represented. I believe the Lord will yet do great things on the on this Caravan site.

I have now got a list of all the children who attend and hope to start visitation quite soon. I trust in the will of the Lord that things regarding the Mission Church will soon be resolved*, and we can go ahead with the Induction Services.

Yours in the Master's Service,

(Signed) James W. Brownlee

* James is speaking here about the replacement mobile home, converted into a Meeting place, and his induction service as pastor, as follows.

To Bring Things Up-To-Date concerning the Mission Caravan

The original Caravan used as a Mission Meeting place from May 1971 was unused for a few months in early 1977, and it suffered some storm damage. In May 1977 Mr. Brownlee obtained an estimate of £950.40 from D. & N. Caravan Services to repair and make good. The MMH Council discussed the different options, and asked Mr. N. T. Barber if he would kindly go and assess the Caravan situation first hand, and give a technical report. He did this and found the ceiling had come down and other matters needing attention. He did a full report with diagram – there isn't space to record it here. He advised: "*I think we should write to Mr.*

Brownlee and give him a copy of the Report, and suggest that he has electricity and water disconnected and the gas cylinder removed so that there is no risk of fire etc."

Recommendations

a. That the present caravan be disposed of and a replacement purchased.

b. That we attempt to recover insurance as a "Write off" claim.

c. That we relinquish the present site on the understanding that we should like a new site, suitable for a 30ft replacement caravan, in the same area.

It was decided to accept these recommendations and the Director, being up in Scotland in September, contacted Londays Caravan Sales and a modern style "Willerby Leven" caravan was chosen at the cost of £850.00. (A deposit was paid, with the remainder to be paid when it is properly sited and connected to services.) With the additional toilet, and some rent it came to almost £1,000. The Lord in His faithfulness answered prayer and in the end it all came in quite quickly. Praise God!

At last we could fix a date for Mr. Brownlee's Induction Service – on Saturday 5th November 1977 (D.V.). The following is the report of this service.

Scottish News

Dedication of New M.M.H. Mission Church
Induction Service of Mr. J.W. Brownlee

On November 5th 1977 the new Mission Church was dedicated to the glory of God, and Mr. J.W. Brownlee was inducted to the Pastorate. It was a moving service, conducted by Pastor Hector Hall, MMH Director, with the hymns chosen by Mr. Brownlee. *"All people that on earth do dwell"* was heartily sung, then Pastor Whyte led in prayer. Mrs. Whyte sang two beautiful solos, *"His Love has no limit"* and *"Help me present the Gospel"*. *"The Church's One Foundation"* was sung by the congregation, followed by the reading from *2 Timothy chapter 4*.

A report was given of the guidance of God, in the provision of the new MMH Mission Church, in answer to believing prayer. The Mission to Mobile Homes Council had this burden very much on their hearts.

The congregation was upstanding as Pastor Hall asked Mr. Brownlee three questions: -

Will you promise to preach the whole counsel of God?
Will you tend and care for the flock?
Will you do the work of an evangelist?

He responded: "*I will, with God's help*". Prayer was then offered that God's grace and spirit would be upon our brother in his new ministry.

"*Glorious things of Thee are spoken*" was sung and the Rev. James Whitted brought the charge to the new minister from *2 Timothy 4:1*: "*Preach the Word*". He gave an appropriate and powerful message. The simple, but impressive service came to a close with the singing of "*Guide me O Thou Great Jehovah*" and the Benediction. Mr. Alex Brady assisted at the organ.

Mrs. Brownlee and the ladies prepared a lovely tea, for which Pastor Brownlee said the Grace, and we all enjoyed good fellowship. Greetings were received from the Council of the Mission, the Rev. C. Gellaitry, Mr. & Mrs. A. Marshall, and Mr, Alex Ritchie.

On the Lord's Day, Pastor Brownlee conducted the Sunday School and addressed the children. At the 11.30 a.m. adult Service, Pastor Hall expounded *Matthew 16:18* "*Christ is the Master Builder of His Church*".

Children's Mission Report

Greetings in the Saviour's Name! Truly, the Lord has been blessing here at the Pentland Mission Church.

The Children's Mission concluded on Friday night after three weeks. Mr. Bilton of the Mission to Village Children conducted the Mission and was very pleased with the consistent attendance. The average attendance was about twenty. On two occasions we had twenty-five children packed in. The children were well behaved on the whole. Time will only tell what seed has been sown in needy hearts.

I would value your prayers for one boy, Andrew is his name, and he had not attended Sunday School. However, after the Mission he got a Bible for a prize for answering questions. He has now started coming to Sunday School along with his sister.

Mr. Bilton runs a Summer Camp and some of the children would like to go, to hear more of the Word of God. If anyone would like to sponsor a child, and help make it financially possible for them to attend the camp, please contact Pastor J.W. Brownlee, Tel...

We would say "To God be the Glory for what he has done thus-

far" and we believe the best is yet to be.

Yours in the Lord's Service,

Pastor James W. Brownlee.

Family Service
We had the Family Service on Sunday 18th December. Some of the parents did come along. We had a good service, Praise the Lord!

Carol Singing
We went Carol Singing on Tuesday 20th December on the Site and we were very well received. We gave out invitations to the Christmas Eve Service along with a Gospel tract. A group from the Tabernacle Baptist Church joined us.

J.W.B.

Scotland: Anniversary Blessings!
The Lord has been blessing here at the Pentland Mission Church. We had a very good weekend of Services. On the week leading up to the Church Anniversary we had a special week of CHILDRENS MEETINGS... many new contacts were made with boys and girls, who had not been to the Mission Church before.

On Saturday 13th May 1978 we had a special Anniversary Rally at which Rev. James Whitted was the guest speaker, and Mr. Colin Williams with his guitar brought the message in song. Some of the older girls came to the meeting and thoroughly enjoyed it.

On Sunday 14th we continued the Anniversary weekend with a family service. We had 24 packed into the Caravan Church (16 children and 8 adults). All of these came from the Caravan Sites, except myself, my wife and Mr. Bilton, who was the speaker on this occasion. The LORD has indeed been blessing and we believe the best is yet to be. We also held an evening service at 6:30; again, some of the older Sunday School children came along with Mr. Angus. I brought the word at this service speaking on 'Jonah'.

Pastor J. Brownlee

Mr. Brownlee ministered faithfully for four and a half years, ably supported by his first wife Ina, until her serious illness meant that he had to lay down the work. Mrs. Brownlee, too, served very consistently until that ill health prevented her. The Mission did appreciate all that she did.

One of his referees correctly summed him up:

Jim is a sound Bible-believing Christian with a deep sense of responsibility to see completed, any task he undertook.

A few years later, after his marriage to Jean, his second wife, James joined Hector in Gospel outreach on the Nivensknowe, Pentland, and Straiton Park. There they met dear Mrs. Londi, whose husband was in sympathy with the Mission's work, and their son Enzo who had attended the Mission's Sunday School in the early days of the Mission.

34 Moulton Evangelical Church

Before we move forward in the unfolding MMH story, and the expansion of the work in the 1980s, we must look back in time to Prince of Wales Row, and tell a little of 'EVANGELISM at the PUB', for the house we lived in had originally been a Public House. The work and witness to Christ through the power of the HOLY SPIRIT of GOD, was the motivation of what was happening there!

The following is based upon the report that I wrote, which appeared in '*Faith & Victory*', the MMH Newsletter, dated May 1974.

MOULTON EVANGELICAL CHURCH
Opening & Dedication Service of
"The Meeting Room"

The meeting, on Saturday 20th April 1974, began with the singing of "*To God be the glory*" and with prayer, after which Mrs. Ann Hall opened the Meeting Room. Pastor Hector Hall welcomed friends from different churches who had joined us for this happy occasion. Greetings were received from various parts of the British Isles. Although the number attending was a little disappointing, those who did attend were whole-hearted in their support.

The building was dedicated to God as a house of prayer where God's presence might be known; that souls might be saved; and the Word of God faithfully preached in the power of the Holy Spirit.

Mr. Hall told in his report how God had given promises in answer to prayer and fasting: *1 Chronicles 28:20* "He will not fail thee …until thou hast finished all the work" (the promise given on 7th January 1973 and repeated on 7th February 1974) and *Ecclesiastes 8:12* "It shall be well with them that fear God". He paid tribute to three people in particular who had assisted him: Mr. Duncan Black, of Balloch, Scotland who gave up a week's holiday to do the roof; Mr. Nigel Barber, who spent many hours rewiring and seeing to the electrical supply; and Mr. Tony Stewart who helped with the new floor.

We give praise to the Lord for his provision of 25 folding chairs that were previously used by the Manchester Crusade led by Rev. Stephen Olford. We thank Mr. Steele of Macclesfield, who arranged for us to have them, and for the *"Operation Mobilization"* workers who brought them down to Moulton. We also thank all who helped our brother Adrian to scrape and re-varnish them. Last but not least we thank Mr. Paul Robinson who has painted a nice new 'Notice Board' giving times of services, now displayed in Overstone Road.

A summary of the Opening Address by Rev. B. Lambert, Pastor of Wellingborough Baptist Tabernacle

"We have reached a commencement with the opening of this Meeting Hall, today. It is good to meet people with a passion and concern for souls. I like to meet zealous people. Mr. Hall has shown unwavering faith and tenacity of purpose. We should hold in high esteem those who labour in the Gospel. We have launched out into something very wonderful today."

Pastor Lambert then went on to apply *Psalm 132* to the Pastor and people of Moulton Evangelical Church. "Sleepless nights" until I find a place for the Lord – *verses 4 & 5*. He referred to "David, and all his afflictions" – *verse 1*. He warned the fellowship of the diabolical assaults of the evil one, and exhorted us to preach a full-orbed message of the Gospel. There was a PRAYER for the Lord to fill the building with His presence: "Arise, O Lord, into Thy rest" – *verse 8*. The Lord must be in it – a place for presenting Christ in His Fullness. He stressed the importance of the weekly Prayer Meeting. Everything depends upon Communication from the Living Head. He told us that the Church he was with for 7 years in Argentina decided everything in the prayer meeting – the Theocratic form of Church government.

Pastor Lambert shared how Christ in the midst can make His will known. In *Acts 13* the whole Church was involved in the separating of Paul and Barnabas for God's work – the whole church went with them. We have the mind of Christ. We pray that you may have revelations of the will of the Lord as the Church goes forward. The Lord is building His Church – that church must conquer. The Lord Jesus is not a spectator. He IS the BUILDER. He is the Architect. The Lord has a plan. We give glory to God for giving our brother His plan, our prayers will be with him: "Here will I dwell" – *verse 14.*

Finally, a PROVISION "I will satisfy her poor with bread" – *verse 15.* Why, people may ask, another meeting? Many people are becoming selective and discerning: they are going where the food is!

After the singing of "*My hope is built on nothing less*",
Mr. F. J. Hodges of Reynard Way Evangelical Church closed the
meeting with prayer.

35 Sharon Moira Hall

Sharon Moira, the second daughter of Hector and Ann Hall, was born on 13th April 1966 at Irvine Central Hospital, Ayrshire, Scotland, with Ann's Mum, Mrs. Helen Creighton, lovingly helping at their home prior to and after the birth. Sharon moved with her parents to Moulton, Northampton in October 1967, when she was just one year and six months old. As she grew up she was a bright, intelligent, cheerful little girl. At three years of age she could talk, and use long words in their proper context. At the dinner table, conversation was to say the least very lively in the Hall household. On a Saturday morning she would go to the local Library with her Dad and sister Carolyn and get books out, while Mum was getting Dinner ready, the Library being just along the road.

At this time, we had the Christian Life Book Service in operation, so new Christian books and Bibles were readily available to read. Ann used to read to the girls not only Christian books, but also the current Ladybird books. One book in particular gave Sharon nightmares, so I used to get up out of bed, go into her bedroom, and give her a kiss and a cuddle and say, "It is alright Sharon, Daddy is here", and she would go back to sleep!

At Moulton County Primary School Carolyn was studious and worked hard, and her teacher was pleased with her. But when Sharon moved up into the same Class it was not plain sailing for the teacher. *Why?* you may well ask! Sharon was blessed with a photographic and retentive memory: once she heard a thing she remembered it. So, she would talk during the lesson to Dr. Campling's son Marcus. However, when the teacher asked Sharon a question she always seemed to have the right answer. Each term Ann and I had to attend the Parent/Teacher evening. "Sharon talks too much in class", said her teacher. Mrs. Campling had the same problem regarding her son Marcus – but of course as they grew up they learned to pay attention.

As we lived by faith in God to meet our material needs, money was scarce, but we nonetheless refused to look to the Welfare State for our support. However, *God answered prayer* concerning clothing for Carolyn and Sharon, and Ann always had them turned out smartly dressed. There was a lady in Ann's parents' Church, whose daughter was a similar age to Carolyn, and who kindly sent on Marks & Spencer children's clothes, which were bright in colour and attractive. They were of such good quality that Sharon also wore the dresses, and they were finally given away to other children.

As *Carolyn and Sharon* grew up, their Scottish aunts, *Joy* and *Evangeline*, were very kind in seeing that the girls were smartly dressed, and thus the Lord provided.

Carolyn and Sharon got on so well with their school friends that they came regularly to our home on a Thursday evening for '***Children's Special***', run by Ann, and Sheila Gordon, a fellow-member of Grafton Square Evangelical Church. In this meeting there were always lively Christian Choruses, Bible reading, Memory Verse and Bible Story. A *Memory Verse* was written out on a piece of card to be taken home and learned. One of the first of these was *Jonah 2:9* "Salvation is of the LORD." I believe Sharon began to get a vision for this type of work through '*Children's Special*'. At Christmas they had a Christmas party of much joy. On one occasion as the children left to go home after the meeting, and were walking down the passage to the front door, a little boy amusingly said, "This is Hector's House!" – the name of a popular children's T.V. programme at that time.

Other meetings were held at Prince of Wales Row: A Monthly MMH Prayer Meeting, with vital prayer and intercession for the Mission workers and the salvation of people on the different Sites. There was an 8.15pm After-Church Meeting for local Christians, and unsaved people heard the Gospel of God's grace.

Then the outside Coal-Shed at our home was transformed into a Meeting Room to seat 24 people for Moulton Evangelical Church, of which I was the Honorary Pastor. There was a Sunday Morning Worship Service, a Sunday Evening Gospel Service, and mid-week Prayer Meeting and Bible Study.

Sharon's Conversion
It was at such a Meeting on Sunday evening 3rd August 1975 that as Sharon heard the Gospel once again, God's Holy Spirit worked in her

heart to respond to the Gospel of Christ. I had preached from *John's Gospel Chapter 4* on 'Christ the Life-Giver.' Following the Service, she told me that she had asked 'Christ to forgive her sins, and come into her life.' That was the start. She had been taught God's Word from an early age, but now she accepted God's Word of Truth, and claimed the promises of God for herself. She had a keen mind, and grew in the Lord. Carolyn came to faith in Christ a year later, and so Ann and I praised God for His blessing and answered prayer.

Later, in 1977, when God moved us to Benington Sea End, near Boston, Lincolnshire, Carolyn and Sharon attended Old Leake Secondary School. One of the teachers was Dennis Ottaway who was Lay Pastor at Boston Baptist Church. Sharon benefited from having different teachers for different subjects, which broadened her education. The Giles Secondary School awarded her the **Progress Prize** for 1978, and she was made a Prefect. On leaving School she continued her studies at Lincoln College of Further Education, and stayed during the week with our dear friend Margaret Birt.

The MMH had a stall at the Filey Christian Holiday Crusade, through the recommendation of Mr. Peter Assheton our Chairman. It was while attending the excellent Youth Meetings that Sharon was challenged about full-time Missionary Service. She was baptized with others at Boston Baptist Church: although converted at 9 years of age, we thought it better for her to wait for baptism until she was in her teens.

After much prayer Sharon felt led to apply to the Bible College of Wales, Swansea. I visited the College regularly each year, and gave a Bible Lecture to the students, and took a Missionary Meeting on behalf of the MMH. But it was Sharon's own decision to go to B.C.W., as it was affectionately known.

An unsolicited comment:
"Just a little note to say how lovely it was to meet Sharon when we were at the College recently (Bible College of Wales, Swansea). She's a sweet little girl (4 Foot 10 inches!) and the College is very fond of her. We'll pray about her future and what the Lord wants her to do with her life. Every blessing on your work."

In Him,

Bessie Dryers, F.E.B.V.
(Fellowship for Evangelizing Britain's Villages)

Sharon enjoyed lectures given by the Director, Rev. Samuel Howells M.A., and the special Prayer Sessions. She appreciated the teaching given by Dr. Mowbray, and Mr. Davis, who had experienced Revival in Africa. She also enjoyed fellowship with Pearl Temple, Leader of the Women Students, and of course with fellow-students. Mr. Sam Docherty's visit to the College showed Sharon the need for the Gospel amongst boys and girls in Poland. He represented Child Evangelism Fellowship (C.E.F.), working in Eastern Europe. God also used two students at the College who were from Poland to speak to Sharon of the need there.

After applying to C.E.F. she spent two useful years doing Child Evangelism in Cornwall and in Scotland. She then spent twelve years serving the Lord in Poland. The first part of this time was with C.E.F., working with Mr. Czesław Bassara (Director) in taking Children's Gospel Missions and in training Sunday School teachers 'How to teach the Bible Effectively' in Churches and among the Gypsies, in many places in southern Poland.

The second part of Sharon's time in Poland was spent serving the Baptist Church in Bielsko-Biała with Pastor Greg, where she was used of the Lord in teaching the children and young people God's Word of Truth.

Sadly, Sharon had to leave this work in Poland to return home due to her serious heart condition. She was never one to take the "easy road", so she took on a part-time secretarial job at the Pilgrim Hospital, Boston, for Lincolnshire County Council, in her spare time supporting the young people of Bethel Baptist Church, Billinghay. Sharon initiated the provision of free Scriptural *"Words of Life"* calendars for Eastern European students in the computer room of Boston Public Library, as the Lord directed.

She had used a heart defibrillator even while she was in Poland, but now she needed another operation. She was admitted to the Pilgrim Hospital, and then after a couple of weeks she was transferred to Glenfield Hospital, Leicester, where she had the operation, before being returned to the Pilgrim Hospital.

She then returned home and was very cheerful, but the following day, 27th April 2006, she collapsed in the bathroom and died – rather, she went to be with her Lord. Ann and I were shattered, and poor Carolyn was away in America with her husband Ian. I believe God wanted Sharon – so *like* JESUS – to be *with* JESUS in Heaven. This occurred just after Sharon's 40th birthday.

At her Thanksgiving Service on Friday 5th May a full Bethel Baptist Church, Billinghay, showed how much she was loved and esteemed. People came from all over the U.K. and greetings were received from Poland. Pastor J. Mansfield conducted the service and preached with liberty, and Peter Cotton, the Church's evangelist, prayed movingly and thanked God for her loving and dedicated life. Carolyn gave a loving and personal tribute to her younger sister, on behalf of her parents and family.

A Postscript: A Muslim couple, to whom Sharon had witnessed, turned up just as the service was about to start with a Red Rose. May they come to know the Saviour!

Sharon's life of Christian service merits a fuller account in the future, God Willing.

36   Changes were coming, but first – a Campaign!

At the Opening Service for Moulton Evangelical Church (Chapter 34) Pastor Bernard Lambert had warned us of the diabolical assaults of the evil one. We did indeed experience the serious opposition of Satan, but after prayer and fasting the Lord showed us how to deal with the matter, and He gave us the victory. Then in mid 1976, after nine years in Moulton, through scripture and other circumstances, especially the expanding work of the Mission, the Lord showed us that attention was needed to the future of the work, and on a number of fronts.

So, we waited on the Lord and considered a new area in which to be based. The Lord said 'no' to Norfolk, so where *did* the Lord want us?   At the same time, Moulton Evangelical Church would need a new meeting place.

But in the mean time we had as a Church organized:

MOULTON VILLAGE

ONE WAY ⬆ CAMPAIGN

Saturday, 10th July -
Thursday, 22nd July, 1976

led by MR. LESLIE VAYRO & TEAM
from Birmingham Bible Institute

The following, from our August 1976 report, reveals what a big step of faith this was for a small Church, and what God accomplished.

August 1976.

Psalm 34:3
O magnify the LORD with me, and let us exalt His name together.

We desire to record some answers to prayer, which MAGNIFY the LORD'S NAME, to whom all the glory is due; and to encourage our Prayer Partners who have been faithful at the Throne of Grace.

Moulton Evangelical Church

Report of the **One Way Campaign** conducted by the Team of Students from the Birmingham Bible Institute (B.B.I.), and led by Mr. Leslie & Mrs. Peggy Vayro, on 10th – 22nd July 1976.

CHAPPELL HOUSE A very good meeting was conducted by the team in this senior citizens' house. One lady trusted in the Lord, another re-affirmed, her faith in God, and one other is near the Kingdom.
We praise God!

ONE WAY CLUB An average of 50 Children attended eight special children's meetings in Moulton Primary School. Six Children asked Christ to be their Saviour. Please pray for these 'babes in Christ' that they may grow in grace and knowledge of the Lord. Please pray for the Parents and friends who heard the Gospel faithfully presented on the Parents Night.

OPEN-AIR MEETINGS The first was held outside the Cardigan Arms/Barlow Lane corner on Saturday morning. The village knew the team had arrived! There was a clear presentation of the Gospel of Christ and the need to repent, before it was too late! Passers-by received tracts and invitations to the meetings.

THE GROSVENOR CENTRE, Northampton. A number listened to the Gospel and a large number of tracts were handed out. Pray for God to bless the seed. Pray for a lady, mixed up in her beliefs, whom Les Vayro counselled. Pray for a newsvendor who Dave spoke to, who read our tracts instead of selling his papers! Pray for a Polish Roman Catholic who Dennis witnessed to.

WESTON FAVELL INDOOR SHOPPING CENTRE Many Saturday afternoon shoppers were curious about Tony's work on the sketch board: they listened to the Gospel of Salvation in the message and testimonies by the spoken word, and in Sue's singing of Salvation. Pray for a lady who had been influenced by a false cult, and who was deeply challenged by the spirit-filled messages. Also pray for a Scotsman who was under conviction. One or two Christians came up and introduced themselves.

YOUTH COFFEE BAR This brought in a number off the streets who usually visit the Pubs. Two Christian Couples from B.B.I. Birmingham sang beautifully the message of Salvation in Christ, accompanied by guitar. They certainly knew how to communicate the Gospel to young people. They came in at the last minute, as Mrs. Alison Clarke, who had expected to sing with her husband Philip, was involved in the terrible bus/transporter crash at Isham. She had a remarkable deliverance, and was very composed when I saw her the next day at home being well looked after by her husband. Please remember Alison in prayer as she gets over the bruising and shock

FILM NIGHT – Meet the Team! The film 'A Thief in the Night' was not well attended (Montreal Olympics a distraction?) but one young man, who had attended church a fortnight previously, was counselled after the film. Please pray for him as he has problems.

THE FINAL MEETING in the Guide Hall was a good meeting, with some of the interested young people present who had been given Bibles. There were also visitors from other Churches. The Gospel was again clearly presented.

Indeed – To God Be The Glory Great Things He Hath Done!

VISITATION Prior to the 'One Way Campaign', Church members distributed Campaign leaflets to 1,200 homes in Moulton Village. Good contacts were made. The team faithfully visited the families of all of the children who had attended the meetings.

FOLLOW-UP Pray for members of Moulton Evangelical Church as they follow-up the contacts made.

FELLOWSHIP The Team were given hospitality by church members and we were mutually enriched by fellowship in the furtherance of the Gospel of God. We say a warm thank-you to the ladies and to the team for their Christ-like Ministry and fellowship amongst us. Only ETERNITY will fully reveal all that has been accomplished.

Pastor H. Hall. Hon. Minister.

SATURDAY, 10th JULY
at 6.15 p.m.   Welcome
in The Guide Hall, Barlow Lane
(opposite The Post Office)

SUNDAYS, 11th & 18th JULY
at 11.15 a.m.   Family Worship
in The Guide Hall
at 6.30 p.m.   Team Testifies
Meeting Hall, Prince of Wales Row

MONDAY, 12th JULY —
         WEDNESDAY, 14th JULY
at 6 p.m. - 7 p.m.   Children's Special
in Moulton Primary School

THURSDAY, 15th JULY
at 7 p.m.   Parent's Night

MONDAY, 19th JULY —
           THURSDAY, 22nd JULY
at 2.30 p.m. - 3.30 p.m.   Holiday Special
in Moulton Primary School

TUESDAY, 13th JULY
at 8 p.m.   Youth Coffee Bar
Musical Group
in The Guide Hall

SATURDAY, 17th JULY
at 7 p.m.   Young Teens Night
Film etc.
in The Guide Hall

TUESDAY, 20th JULY
at 7.30 p.m.   Meet the Team
presenting :
Jesus—"The Way, The Truth and The Life"
in The Guide Hall

THURSDAY, 22nd JULY
at 7.30 p.m.   Final Rally
in The Guide Hall
A Hearty Welcome !

arranged by
MOULTON EVANGELICAL CHURCH

Ann's Child Minding
An answer to prayer during our early years in Moulton

Ann waited upon the Lord about the possibility of doing some work from home to earn a few pounds to help the family's financial situation, as first Carolyn and then Sharon became pupils at Moulton Primary School. She did not want to take on anything that would deflect from her priority as a mother in bringing up our two girls and supporting her husband.

One day she answered a knock at the door: it was the Baptist Pastor's wife.   Ann welcomed her in and gave her a cup of tea, whereupon she revealed that she wished to return to teaching and needed someone to look after her son Jamie, who was then sixteen months old. "I feel you are just the right person to do it – and I will pay you, of course." Ann was excited when she told me, because God had answered her prayers – our prayers – and nobody else knew.   We had to obtain permission and then registration from the local authority; the house had to be inspected by the Fire Brigade for safety, and health checks were also carried out.

Carolyn and Sharon loved Jamie (as did Ann & Hector) as they didn't have a brother – he was so full of life; so unpredictable and likeable. He turned up one morning, prior to school as usual, with a screwdriver. His Mum said, "I can't get Jamie to hand it over. I'm frightened of what he might do to your furniture." Ann calmly said, "Don't worry – I know what to do." She then gave Jamie another toy to play with, and he meekly gave up the screwdriver. Is that what is meant by 'child-psychology'? After Jamie and his family moved away Ann also lovingly looked after one other little boy.

37 Zion Evangelical Chapel
(*formerly* Moulton Evangelical Church)

As a family we enjoyed ten memorable years in Moulton, Northamptonshire. These years were spent in taking the Gospel of Christ to people on different Mobile Home Parks in the County, and to some in Bedfordshire; also among the Gypsies in the Thrapston and Burton Latimer area. Spent, too, in ministering the word and Gospel of Christ in different churches and chapels as well as at Moulton Evangelical Church. We made many friends.

After nine years the Lord began to intimate – as the Mission to Mobile Homes was expanding – that we needed to move to pastures new. But where? We happened to see in the 'Exchange & Mart' magazine a bungalow for sale at Sea End near Boston, Lincolnshire – an area completely new to us – at a price we could possibly afford with a reasonable mortgage. We then went to see it, and to visit the town of Boston and the surrounding area.

We now have to *change gear* in the story, because in our moving house, a **new meeting place**, i.e. venue, would be needed for the Moulton Evangelical Church. At this time the fellowship had been meeting for the previous three years in the Meeting Room in the garden at the rear of our home in Prince of Wales Row, and in our house before that. What happy fellowship we enjoyed.

As we waited on God in prayer there appeared in the "*Chronicle & Echo*" newspaper, the following advertisement:

FOR SALE
Methodist Chapel, High Street, Weston Favell £1,250

Would this be the answer? It was 2½ miles from Moulton Village – would people be willing to travel the distance? As we continued to wait on the Lord, a Christian Couple, who knew of our work and witness for Christ, suddenly said out of the blue that they were willing to put up £1,000. This seemed to be an indication from the LORD that we should seriously consider the matter.

We called Special Church Meetings on 1st and 9th September 1976, at which it was decided to put in an offer for £1,000, but this was turned down. The Church then made a revised offer of £1,250, and had a survey done. A deposit of £125 was paid to the Estate Agents, Beattie Son and Leslie Ltd. It was decided to call the building Zion Evangelical Chapel, once purchased. However, the building had first to be advertised on the Open Market for seven days, and if no further offer was made, then our purchase of the building could go ahead. (A Dancing School did put up a higher offer. However, they didn't get the necessary Planning Permission.)

At a Special Church Meeting held on 16th December 1976 at the Overstone Road home of Tony and Marina Stewart, Mr. A. Renton opened in prayer. It was stated that the surveyor's report revealed that "the building was worth more", and Mr. T. Stewart (Hon. Treasurer) proposed that we make an increased offer of £1,400: this was seconded by Pastor H. Hall, and unanimously agreed. This offer was finally accepted – **Praise God**! Church members then worked exceedingly hard to repaint and refurbish the whole of the inside of the chapel in the weekday evenings during the early months of 1977.

Opening Thanksgiving Services

Zion Evangelical Chapel was opened to the Glory of God with Thanksgiving Services on Saturday 11th and Sunday 12th June 1977.

"Great is the LORD and Greatly to be Praised," said Pastor Hector Hall, as he read *Psalm 48* at the commencement of the Opening Service in the afternoon. The good congregation then sang, *"To GOD be the GLORY"*. After this, came a time of Praise and Prayer for God's Presence and blessing to be known in this Chapel. The Pastor gave a report of God's leading and guiding to this point in time.

Pastor Bernard Lambert, a good friend of the pastor, read the second lesson from the *Prophecy of Haggai Chapter 1*. Then we sang the hymn *"How Firm a Foundation, ye saints of the Lord"*, after which the Rev. David Alcock of Wellingborough preached an appropriate, stirring message, from:

> *Haggai 1:8* "Go up to the mountain, and bring wood, and build the house; and I will take pleasure in it, and I will be glorified, saith the LORD."

At 7:15 pm the Cranfield Youth Choir took the whole service, singing Spiritual songs interspersed with Scripture and words of Christian testimony. This brought a challenge to all of those present to know Christ as Saviour and Lord of life. Truly the gospel of the grace of God was proclaimed in word and in song. The Choir was warmly thanked for coming all the way from Bedfordshire; light refreshments were kindly provided by the ladies, and fellowship enjoyed.

115

On the Lord's Day at the 11:15 am Service, The Rev. Calvin Ritchie of Milton Keynes faithfully expounded God's Word from *2 Corinthians 4*, and at the 6 pm Evening Service he preached the Gospel with liberty from *1 Peter 2:24*, with visitors attending the services.

So ended a memorable weekend of blessing.

Pastor and Mrs. Hall, Carolyn and Sharon – Farewell Tea

Mr. Tony Stewart, Church Treasurer, on behalf of the Fellowship, presented Pastor Hall with a copy of *"The History of Christianity"* – a Lion Handbook, which was later signed by members. Mr. Paul Robinson, Elder in Zion Chapel, sincerely thanked Pastor Hall for his faithful ministry of the Word over the past five-and-a-half years in Moulton and now at Weston Favell, which ministry was much appreciated. He said that God had given His servant promises which had been wonderfully fulfilled concerning the new Chapel building, and the salvation of souls in the Mission's work (MMH). He also paid warm tribute to Mrs. Ann Hall's ministry.

On behalf of Mrs. Hall and the girls, Hector thanked the Church for their surprise Tea, and kind words, and for the book gift, which he said he would look forward to reading. He went on to say that he believed that God would continue to bless the Church, and he assured the Fellowship of their prayers.

38   Going East to Boston

When we moved from Moulton, Northamptonshire to Sea End, Benington, four and a half miles from historic town of the original Boston – in Lincolnshire, *Rusty*, our cat, sat in the bottom of the car. The excitement of moving – and the moving of the car – caused her to quickly fall asleep. Carolyn and Sharon had made sure she was on board, and not left behind. What a change from a walled back garden in an end terraced road, to an open garden with fields all around, and rows of vegetables, sometimes cabbages, at other times, cauliflowers.

Out of the car, Rusty crouched down to start with, and then in time she enjoyed walking down the vegetable avenues. Every time we returned home, she came to meet us. One night on returning home in the car, two hedgehogs scampered across the lawn. So much for wild life: more yet to be discovered.

Boston was famous for being the birthplace of **John Foxe**, author of

"Foxes book of Martyrs" (*Acts and Monuments*). In the 1600s Boston was truly a Protestant town. The **Rev. John Cotton** was Vicar of St. Botolph's Church, known as The Stump – it probably got its name in the early days from its unfinished Tower. People came from many miles around to hear his faithful Bible preaching long before the days of motor cars, and before he went with other people known as the Pilgrim Fathers to help found Boston, Massachusetts, in America. Boston, England, celebrates John Cotton's famous historical connections with the U.S.A. but sadly does not major on the Protestant Bible Message.

In recent years, letters I have written to the local Press have not been printed, or even answered. Why is this? The Ecumenical Movement is the cause of this. "Unity" is considered everything today, but the Truth of God's Holy Word is more important and must prevail, that is, the Authority of the Bible. There ought to be a monument to John Foxe in Boston, as he is one of Boston's most famous sons.

Another famous resident who born and brought up in Boston, and lived near the docks, was the poet **Jean Ingelow**, who wrote the hymn, "*And didst Thou love the race that loved not Thee?*" But she is more generally remembered for her epic poem, *The High Tide On The Coast Of Lincolnshire* (1571). It has the lines, "Men say it was a stolen tyde – The Lord that sent it, HE knows all." How true – declaring the Sovereignty of God over His Creation (see *Genesis Chapter 1*).

Perhaps this is the place to clarify who is a true Christian. Briefly, a *true* Christian is someone who realises that he or she is a lost sinner on the road to hell, but who has *repented* of his or her sins. Such have put their trust in Christ Crucified and Risen from the dead, and know their sins have been forgiven through Christ's blood, shed on Calvary, and know that they are going to Heaven, irrespective of denomination. They belong to the Body of Christ, and therefore are in union with Christ and their fellow-believers. As the Apostle Paul says in *Ephesians 4:3* "Endeavouring to keep *(not make)* the unity of the Spirit in the bond of peace." So we *must* personally keep in fellowship with the Lord Jesus, and with fellow-believers, and continue reading and obeying God's inspired Word, living for God's Glory.

Now back to Benington, Boston, Lincolnshire, where we enjoyed the fresh air – but not the crop spraying: you could taste the Metasystox as you came out of the bungalow – and the countryside.

The Lord who guides His servants knows what He is doing. *In Boston*

Town, there were 6 Residential Mobile Home Parks – 5 Traditional and 1 Gypsy – with people <u>unreached</u> with the Gospel of God's love and grace, unknown to us, but known to God. In a few years of patient sowing the LORD would give a few trophies of Saving Grace, and countless people would hear The Gospel of Christ, and many were helped in many ways.

In the early days in the area we started a Monthly Prayer Meeting in our home, "Green Pastures". It was an exciting time for Carolyn and Sharon, who quickly settled in at Giles Secondary School, Old Leake (now Giles Academy). Mr. Dennis Ottaway, one of the teachers there, was Lay Pastor at Boston Baptist Church, until Pastor Mark Warner was inducted. He and another Christian teacher were an encouragement to the girls.

After we had been in the Boston area a year or more, most of the local Mobile Home residents had been visited personally, and had heard that Christ Jesus came into the world to save sinners. They were, I think, surprised that anyone was interested enough to visit them in their homes. The LORD *is* of course more than interested, and He sends His servants to tell them of Salvation.

Then the Lord in His mercy and grace sent a Christian couple to encourage us! **Mr. George and Mrs. Helena Wood**, a retired couple, came from Liverpool to live on the Lea Mobile Home Park. George had been a preacher of the Gospel and Helena was a gifted pianist. They had for a number of years recorded "*Joy Songs*" sung by Helena, who had written many of them, and with a Bible message by George. They were completely in agreement with the Christian ministry of The Mission to Mobile Homes, and with our Basis of Faith.

They graciously allowed us to hold our MMH Monthly Prayer Meeting in their home, as friends who attended lived in Boston town. It was also good to have fellow-believers on the Lea Park who witnessed to the Saviour, and also to have a home to go to for a cup of tea and fellowship after visitation evangelism on the Park. (All this was before the Lord provided Bethany House in Pump Square, Boston, for our MMH Headquarters.) We also held a Christmas Carol Service in their home on at least three occasions, which were a joy to many, and with Helena in her element at the piano – she was Welsh, and musically gifted. Sweet Carols were sung from the heart, uplifting our wonderful Saviour. This prepared the way for Hector to bring a Bible message, centred in Christ,

The Prince of Peace. We would then share a cup of tea and a mince pie, and enjoy sweet fellowship, George graciously welcoming everyone.

Sadly, George was finally taken ill with pneumonia, which he had previously suffered from in Liverpool, and was taken into the Pilgrim Hospital in Boston. There, he was a bright witness, reading his Bible, and a nurse asked him, "Why do you read the Bible, Mr. Wood?" He replied, "It is God's inspired Word." I visited him and read the Word and prayed with him, and took Leana to see him, before the Lord chose to call him home. The Funeral Service was held in the Gospel Hall, in Trinity Street, and was conducted by Mr. Nelson. I was asked to give the message, and words of personal tribute to his godly character, and words of comfort to dear Helena and the family.

Leana, as friends affectionately knew her, found life very hard after George had been called home, and we did our best to help her. She had the unfortunate experience to fall out of bed one morning at 1am, and could not get back into bed, but she nonetheless waited until 8am before she phoned us. We had a difficulty – as our car was out of action – so we started walking down the road, when a passer-by kindly stopped and gave us a lift to Church Road. We walked down to the Lea Park, where Leana was able to use her walking stick to prise open the 'Emergency Door' of her home.

We thus gained entry, and Ann and I helped her back into bed. Ann made her some warm porridge, toast and marmalade, and a welcome cup of tea! While Ann was preparing breakfast, I read *Psalm 84* and prayed with her.

> *Psalm 84:11* "For the LORD God is a Sun and a Shield: the LORD will give grace and glory: no good thing will He withhold from them that walk uprightly."

Leana Moves to Cromer

It was not long after this before Leana revealed to us that she was going to live in a Brethren Senior Citizen's Home in Cromer, Norfolk, of which Mr. Nelson of the Boston Gospel Hall was a trustee. We were sorry to lose Leana, as she quickly went to Cromer. We arranged a Farewell Tea with her friends at our new home in Eastwood Road, Boston, and had to go to Cromer to bring her back for the occasion. It was a wonderful evening, with presentations and flowers, which she greatly enjoyed. She stayed overnight, and we motored her back to Cromer the next day.

She was well looked after, but was quite lonely, in Cromer. Her son,

Rev. George Wood (Junior) and his wife served with the Baptist Seamen's Mission in Baton Rouge, Louisiana, U.S.A. and didn't get over to England very often. We didn't get that way very often either – Cromer is 90 miles from Boston – but when we did, we took her out to the sea front to enjoy the sea air and the lovely Norfolk Coast.

When Leana received her home-call to Heaven, Rev. George Wood, who was her only son, came over for her Funeral Service held at her late husband's graveside at Boston Cemetery. We thank God for her life lived for the Lord, and her love of her Lord. It was also good to renew fellowship with George Junior and his dear wife, and to hear more of their good Gospel work amongst the Seamen. As believers we await the Lord's Return, or His call to Heaven, and re-union with those gone before, who were also, "In Christ" (*2 Corinthians 5:17*).

> *Revelation 5:13b* "BLESSING, and HONOUR, and GLORY and POWER, be unto HIM THAT SITTETH UPON the THRONE, and unto the LAMB for EVER and EVER."

39   First Known Convert in Boston

Phyllis, a lady in her sixties, lived on the Holland Mobile Home Park, Chain Bridge Road, to the west of the town. She had been in Nursing in her younger days in the old Hospital near the Docks, and her husband had since died. Hector contacted her in visitation evangelism in June 1982.

The Holland Park had a nice green, almost the size of a football pitch, in front of the two roads of Mobile Homes. In the summer a few Holiday touring Caravans used this Park, and Phyllis's Mobile Home was situated near the end of the Park. Phyllis listened at her doorstep as Hector spoke to her of her need of Christ as her personal Saviour from sin. She later told her friend Lilly, "I had a man come to my home who told me I was a sinner. I didn't like that!"

We prayed for her salvation, and on a later visit she invited Hector into her home, where he prayed and read *John's Gospel Chapter 3*, explaining the way of Salvation. He up-lifted Christ Crucified who died in her place, shedding His precious blood to make peace with God, so that she could be forgiven her sins. He finished with a prayer of repentance for sin, and faith in Christ, before leaving. When he next met her a week or ten days later she revealed on that previous visit *Christ* had met with her, and before the night was out she had accepted Him into her heart and life as her personal Saviour. Hallelujah!

The next event was a meeting in her home on June 29th 1982, which her friend Lilly also attended, as did our friends George and Helena Wood, and Ann and myself, and also two neighbours. We sang some hymns, prayed, read the Scriptures and George gave the message. It was good for George and Helena to meet Phyllis as they too lived in a Mobile Home over on the Lea Park and were mature Christians who could help Phyllis, as I often had to be away in Scotland, Northern Ireland and Canada. She loved listening to Audio Tapes of William McCrae's Gospel Songs. She regularly attended the MMH Monthly Prayer Meeting, kindly held in George and Helen's home on the Lea Park, this being before Bethany House was opened as the Mission's Headquarters.

This brief report appeared in "FAITH & VICTORY", August 1982

A Good Meeting In New Convert's Home

We had a good meeting on 29th June in the home of a recent convert on the Holland Mobile Home Park, in Boston. Eight people attended – three of them unsaved friends of hers.

The Message from Mr. George Wood was based on John Chapter 9.

We then had a cup of tea, and another hour of Questions and Answers chaired by the Director.

Phyllis had a car so she could and did regularly visit George and Helena. I also introduced her to friends at Pennygate Evangelical Church in Spalding. She later moved to Tattershall Thorpe village and supported Harold Appleyard, who kept the little Methodist Chapel open. Phyllis was keen to serve the Lord and started a Sunday School at the Chapel, attended by boys and girls from the village, and some who were children of R.A.F. personnel serving at Coningsby. She loved the Christian choruses, and taught the children Bible Stories and memory verses, and at Christmas each year put on a Nativity play performed by the children, with parents attending. She and Harold later attended the Opening of Bethany House, the MMH Headquarters in Pump Square, Boston. (See Chapter 41). She desired to be baptized as a believer, in obedience to Christ's command, and was baptized at Coningsby Baptist Church. Pastor Brown conducted the service, which Ann and I attended.

After Harold died she moved to a cottage at Kirton, and then with failing health she moved to a Nursing Home in Stickney where she died, and went to be with her Lord whom she loved and faithfully served. We attended her funeral at Kirton Parish Church. We thank God for her life and bright testimony.

Psalm 16:11 **"In Thy presence is fulness of joy; at Thy right hand there are pleasures for evermore."**

40 Open Door of Opportunity in Ontario, Canada

The following is drawn from the contemporary report, after a significant first Preaching Tour of Ontario, Canada.

THE MISSION TO MOBILE HOMES

'FAITH & VICTORY'   Canadian Supplement

Open Door of Opportunity in Ontario, Canada.

In November 1979 whilst in London I called at Canada House and did some research concerning Mobile Home Parks in Ontario, Canada. Throughout 1980 the Lord kept on bringing Canada to my attention. Was it the Lord's time for me to visit Canada?

Whilst on holiday in Torquay I prayed that the Lord would confirm His will in this matter, particularly as only a few meetings had so far been arranged in Canada. The host at the Guest House revealed to me that he had been to Ontario and had visited a Mobile Home Park. On the Lord's Day morning the Lord drew my attention during my quiet time to *Isaiah 30:21*: "Thine ears shall hear a word behind thee, saying, This is the way, walk ye in it". That evening in Upton Vale Baptist Church the acting minister took 'Guidance' as his subject. He said, "A clear vision of what we are to do and where we are to go …we must be ready to act. God wants the best for His children. We must sometimes STEP OUT IN FAITH".

God confirmed that word in Boston Baptist Church at the end of August. "We must step out in faith" was twice repeated. Also, a hymn was given:

Have faith in God, my heart, Trust and be unafraid:
God will fulfil in every part, Each promise He has made…
God's mercy holds a wiser plan, Than thou canst fully know.

Bryn Austin Rees , 1911-83 © Alexander O. Scott

So that was the Lord's plan for me: to visit Canada and evangelise the Mobile Home people, but as yet my ticket was not booked. The air fare was £200, so I drew £20 from the MMH General Fund account for the deposit. The flights had to be booked within a week. On 2nd September I had a day of prayer and fasting specifically for the air fare. I read part of *Psalm 119*, and *verse 17* spoke to my heart – "Deal Bountifully with thy servant". The Holy Spirit enabled me to plead with God to deal BOUNTIFULLY in this matter, and send to me the remaining money needed for the fare i.e. £180. The Lord's quiet assurance filled my heart that He would answer prayer.

On Saturday 6th September a letter arrived from a complete stranger: "I was very interested to read a copy of '*FAITH & VICTORY*' and to hear that such a clear witness of the Gospel is going forth to those who live in Mobile Homes. Enclosed is a gift from the Lord to help in some way to spread His glorious Gospel". The gift enclosed was £180. *Hallelujah*!

TORONTO BOUND!

Friends of the Church of the Word, Panshanger (Welwyn Garden City), kindly gave me hospitality so as to be near London Airport, and Mr. Street kindly drove me to Heathrow on Monday 13th October. On the Air Canada "Tristar" 31,000 feet over Greenland a Welsh lady in the seat next to me had difficulty in breathing so I had to get the stewardess. On the final part of the journey – having eaten a lovely chicken dinner, sweet and coffee – this lady was ready to talk about the things of God and accepted a John's Gospel, having had the way of Salvation explained to her.

On arrival at Toronto International Airport, there was no one to meet me: my letter had been delayed due to a postal work-to-rule. The Lord undertook, however, and I eventually spent 'Thanksgiving Night' in the Central Y.M.C.A. Outside the streetcars, like the old Glasgow trams, went clanging by till the early hours. Across the square were tall skyscraper buildings, lit up all night.

On the Tuesday morning I went to Toronto Baptist Seminary where the Principal, Dr. Geoffrey Adams, graciously received me. He kindly showed me over the Seminary buildings and the Jarvis Street Church, and introduced me to the staff and students. An extra morning chapel was assigned for me to address. Mr. & Mrs. H. Magee kindly gave me hospitality.

On Wednesday afternoon I went to Kitchener by Gray Coach. A Jewess sitting next to me told me her husband had been in the motion picture business. She didn't find the Christian Faith easy to talk about or accept but listened to my testimony of Christ's saving grace. I then went on to tell her that Jesus is the promised Messiah and quotations from

Isaiah 9 and *53* and *Deuteronomy 18* backed up the claim. Reference was also made to the promised Second Advent of Christ and the need to be ready for His coming. May the Holy Spirit open her eyes and bring her to repentance and faith in Jesus as Lord and Saviour.

On arrival in Kitchener I went to see the Rev. Robert Reading, minister of First Baptist Church, Waterloo. He kindly fixed up accommodation for me with John and Nancy Pomeroy and their daughters Lyn and Sharon. John and Nancy were formerly missionaries in Zambia – John is now deputation secretary for A.E.F. in Canada – and they were a great help to me in every way. That evening I had the privilege of attending a special Church Meeting at First Baptist, Waterloo, as they contemplated the prospect of a new building costing one million Canadian dollars!

Matthew 9:29 "According to your faith be it unto you".

On Lord's Day morning, Mr. Byers who led the Pastor's Bible Class asked me to speak for a few minutes. Greetings were given and I welcomed the opportunity to speak about the work of the Mission.

Martins Park and Sales, North Waterloo.

This Mobile Home Park was situated out of Waterloo on Route 85 towards Elmira. The Gray Coach came to a stop opposite the Park. The site-owner Mr. Howard Martin turned out to be a Christian; he attends 'The Missionary Church'. A plaque on the mantle-piece read 'GOD BLESS OUR HOME'. Mr. Martin gave me permission to visit each home with the good news of Salvation in Christ Jesus. At the first home a Roman Catholic lady told me there had been a bereavement in the family. I assured her of my prayers for the family and told her the Lord Jesus has conquered death. He can meet your need. A Pentecostal believer was met at the next home. Christian tracts were left at those homes where there was no one at home.

A born-again Christian couple Mr. & Mrs. Lorne Martin, who worship at Velvet Hill Baptist Church, had a plaque at the side of their front door clearly printed with *Ephesians 2:8* "FOR BY GRACE ARE YE SAVED THROUGH FAITH". A clear witness to all who call, that salvation is God's free unmerited gift. Mrs. Martin gave me a snack after I had visited every home.

Another lady, Mrs. M., has relations in England. She listened to the way of salvation as I explained it to her, reading different verses from John's Gospel. Please pray that she may read the Word of God and come to faith in the Lamb of God who takes away the sin of the world.

A Roman Catholic woman was encouraged to repent of her sins and trust in Christ for forgiveness and salvation.

Please pray for a lady who said, "In NO WAY would I become a Christian!" I felt led to tell her that Jesus is the way – a new and living way to God – the only way to God. He has shed His precious blood that our sins might be forgiven and that we might have peace with God.

Mrs. M. is a Pentecostal believer. Up in front of her mobile home was clearly to be seen 'TO GOD BE THE GLORY'. She welcomed me in and gave me a cup of coffee, which was much appreciated as it had rained most of the morning. She told me how she had come to know the Lord as her Saviour and then how her husband had been converted. After Bible reading and prayer I went on my way rejoicing giving God the glory for what He had done!

Adventures Living Park

On 17th October I boarded the Gray Coach to Listowel to visit the above Park with its exciting name. It involved a pleasant journey into Mennonite country. The early settlers of this part of Southern Ontario were of German origin. They wear black coats and hats and drive a horse and buggy to market. On arrival at Adventures Living Park it began to rain heavily, and the office was closed. At number six a lady told me she had recently attended a Morning Coffee Bible Study. She accepted Christian literature and referred me to Mr. & Mrs. Hooton who manage the Park and live at number forty-six. Mrs. Hooton and her daughter Nancy were in but did not wish me to call on the people as they had had adverse reaction from one of the residents. They told me however that they had come to know the Lord of recent time and were that very afternoon sending out invitations to special meetings being held in the Pentecostal Church in Listowel. I told them I was glad to know that they were saved and that they had been witnessing to their neighbours. We had prayer together and I suggested they continue to pray for the people and look to the people to come to them and ask questions concerning the hope that they have in Christ.

A young woman in the 'Kentucky Fried Chicken' listened to the Gospel of Jesus (as I sheltered from the elements). She accepted free Christian tracts and gave me a free cup of coffee!

Strathroy - Stranger Than Fiction

I went by VIA RAIL (the Canadian travel company) from Kitchener, changing trains at London, Ontario. This train had three big, heavy carriages, the locomotive engine being part of the first carriage. At each station the guard had to put a square step down as the platforms are not raised as in Britain. On arrival at Strathroy station I crossed the rail line and came around to an Esso Garage on the corner. On asking a motorist the way to the Twin Elms Park. He replied, "You are from England. What part?" I replied "Boston, Lincolnshire." He said, "My father came from Boston, Lincolnshire. He used to live in Fydell Street. You are the first person I have ever come across over here who came from Boston, Lincolnshire!" He then told me to wait while he paid for his Gasoline (*Petrol*). He gave me a lift to the Twin Elms Park and I told him that I was an evangelist, a preacher of the Gospel of Jesus. He told me he was a saved man. He rejoiced in the satisfaction of being a saved man. Yes, the joy and peace through believing in Jesus.

The Twin Elms Mobile Home Park is well laid out with spacious double width Homes and spacious gardens. Mr. A, a Scottish Presbyterian, was a believer. When I explained to him that I was encouraging people to have faith in God and know Jesus Christ as Saviour, he encouraged me, "Keep up the good work!" Many people living on this mobile home estate heard the message of the grace of God, and were given S.G.M. tracts and booklets.

A man originally from Gateshead, England, was ready to talk about the Good News Jesus gives. He received 'Be sure' and 'Honey Bees and Heavenly Blessings' tracts. Mrs. G. said she was a Christian and supported the Anglican Church and Youth for Christ in London.

In the Via Rail Waiting Room a Roman Catholic lady from Siberia, Russia, told me of the atrocities her people had suffered in Siberia twenty years ago. People being taken away and killed. It was all so vivid to her, as if it had only been yesterday. Alas, it is still going on.

Cedar Grove Mobile Home Park, Mississauga.

On returning to Toronto I went to the above Park, where Mrs. Tryon showed me over the latest Mobile Homes. I then was introduced to Mr. & Mrs. F. Pallet, owners of the Park, who were curious about this visitor from the old country, so I had a good opportunity to speak to them of Christ's love and saving grace. Mr. Pallet then kindly drove me in his car around the eighteen-acre site.

I commenced to visit in Third Avenue and prayed that the Lord would lead me to someone who needed Him. I met a Presbyterian lady from Maryhill, Glasgow, who had recently been bereaved of her husband in June. She was appreciative of fellowship and was encouraged to daily read the Word of God, starting in the New Testament. She had an appointment to keep, so time was scarce. However, prayer was offered for God's blessing and comfort before leaving.

A man aged fifty-five to sixty years retorted, "We don't have faith in Christ AT ALL!" then quickly shut the door. Let us take this man upon our hearts and pray him into the kingdom.

Two teenaged girls were challenged about their need of Christ and were given a copy of 'God's Answer'.

"Small matters can, providentially, have important outcomes". Debbie, a young teenager to whom I witnessed as I was about to leave the Park said "Have you called at the Corner Home?" "Yes," I replied "but I received no answer." This led me to call again, where I met Roy and Helene Paul, a Christian Couple, who greatly helped me and gave me gracious hospitality on subsequent preaching Tours. A real answer to prayer! They kindly invited me to have a meal with them and then Roy and I went to their church – Rexdale Alliance Church. It was the mid-week prayer meeting, where I enjoyed the fellowship of God's people. We split up into small groups of seven – this makes it easier for people to take part and they more readily share needs in a small group. Mr. Jim Scorgie, an elder of the Church, kindly invited me to his home for supper, and then drove me back to the Toronto Baptist Seminary.

Memorable Meetings.

A memorable final day of meetings was held in Toronto on Thursday 23rd October 1980. In the morning I was able to share with the keen students of the Toronto Baptist Seminary news of what the Lord has been doing on the four Ontario Mobile Home Parks. In the afternoon of that day I called on Rev. Douglas Graham at the Leprosy Mission office. We had a good time of fellowship.

In the evening it was a joy to renew fellowship with Dr. Eric Gurr, minister of Jarvis Street Baptist Church, and to meet his elders and people. The Jarvis Street Baptist Church graciously gave me the whole meeting to show coloured slides of "Evangelism Among Caravan people" in the British Isles, and a good prayer session followed the well-attended meeting. Our brother Edward Hodges kindly drove me to Toronto

International Airport for the flight home. TO GOD BE THE GLORY!

CONCLUSIONS

An Ontario publication had this to say about TOMATO harvesting: "Harvesting is a continuous operation requiring the picking of the red ripe tomatoes from the vine".

Red *ripe* tomatoes! Yes, Jesus says: "The fields … are white (ripe) already to harvest," (*John 4:35*) *but* "...the labourers are few" (*Matthew 9:37*).

These are the facts:

1.   There does not appear to be a ministry similar to that of The Mission to Mobile Homes in Canada or the U.S.A.

2.   There are, Praise God, a few good 'born again' believers on the Mobile Home Parks in Canada. We must tap this potential to PRAY and get INVOLVED in evangelism.

3.   The door is wide open for Gospel outreach among the Mobile Home People. Jesus says "Behold, I have set before thee an open door" (*Revelation 3:8*).

4.   Please pray that the Lord will prepare Canadian workers.

5.   Hector Hall, MMH Director, will (D.V.) be over again in October 1981 for follow-up on the sites, deputation meetings in Churches and Colleges, and new outreach in the Barrie/Orillia area of Ontario.

February 1981

PUBLISHED BY

THE MISSION TO MOBILE HOMES   Founded 1967
Headquarters: Constituted 1968
"Green Pastures", Sea End, Benington, Boston,
Lincolnshire, England PE22 0DN

An Evangelical, Faith Orientated, Bible Based Missionary Society, working among Mobile Home People.

41   Great Is Thy Faithfulness!

A Council Meeting of the Mission to Mobile Homes was held on 24th September 1983 at Bethel Evangelical Free Church, Leicester, to discuss: Headquarters Project – 8 Pump Square, Boston, Lincolnshire.

A few salient points that were raised in the meeting:

Gifts totalling £9,556 had come in, in answer to the prayers of God's servants, leaving the amount needed to complete the purchase of the premises at £6,944. The Treasurer raised the question of what would happen should the remaining money not come in on time. The Director rejected seeking a mortgage, and said that he was confident that the Lord would supply all that was needed in time to purchase. He was praying for some large gifts: he had fasted and prayed to that end, and had been resting on the promise:

> *Jeremiah 33:3* "Call unto me, and I will answer thee, and show thee great and mighty things, which thou knowest not."

<u>In the Providence of God</u>, a letter came in a few days later with two cheques to a total value of £7,000 – just the amount that was needed. We did indeed greatly PRAISE THE LORD!

<u>We were further tested</u> when our Solicitor informed us that we would need to find a further £700 pounds for land charges, as the building would not be exclusively for residential use. As I prayed about this, the LORD spoke to me through *Psalm 145:16* "Thou openest Thine hand, and satisfieth the desire of every living thing." *Verse 19* says, "He will fulfil the desire of them that fear Him: He also will hear their cry, and will save them."

So, God graciously provided!

The Lord also answered prayer in the granting of the planning permission needed to hold Christian Meetings at 8 Pump Square, in spite of opposition.

All Praise and Glory to our Great and Faithful God!

Report of The Opening Service at Bethany House, MMH H.Q.
(From 'Faith & Victory', MMH Newsletter, December 1984)

Friends of the Mission to Mobile Homes from Churches in Norfolk, Cambridgeshire and Lincoln packed Bethany House, 8 Pump Square, Boston, on Saturday 6th October 1984. They gave glory to God for the wonderful way He had provided this three-storey building in the centre of the town, in answer to believing prayer and fasting in the name of Jesus.

Pastor Hector Hall, Director of the Mission, conducted the service and recounted the Faithfulness of God to His promises (*Jeremiah 35:5*; *Psalm 145:16 & 19*). He also paid tribute to Mr. N. T. Barber, who had installed the Fire Alarm System, and to the team of Mission helpers who had decorated the whole of the ground and first floor rooms.

The building was then dedicated to the glory of God, and prayer was offered that many precious souls might find Christ as Lord and Saviour.

Mr. J. Neville Knox, President of the MMH, paid tribute to the faith and vision of the Director and his wife. He said it was a privilege to be here on this special occasion (he and Mrs. Knox had come from Leicester, where he was in the middle of a Mini Mission). He then gave an excellent address from *Matthew 15:32*, with a challenge to have real compassion – like the Lord Jesus – for the lost on the Mobile Home Parks (and elsewhere), and to realise that they will perish unless they are lovingly reached with the Gospel of Jesus Christ.

We sang, *"How I Praise Thee, Precious Saviour"*, with its lovely chorus;

> *Channels only, blessed Master,*
> *But with all Thy Wondrous power,*
> *Flowing through us, Thou canst use us*
> *Every day and every hour.*

Mr. D. G. Hayden, MMH Honorary Treasurer, then closed the meeting in prayer.

The Mission Council met earlier in the day under the Chairmanship of Mr. P. C. Assheton.

The Water of Life

We take it for granted that we have running water in our houses. We have only to turn the tap on to get water, but only a few centuries ago, it was not so.

An historical note: there had once literally been a Pump at the centre of <u>Pump Square</u>, and a supply of clean fresh water that could be purchased. In Bible times there used to be "Water Sellers". As Isaiah the Prophet records:

> *Isaiah 55:1* "Ho, every one that thirsteth, come ye to the waters, and he that hath no money; come ye, buy …without money and without price."

In this, Isaiah stresses that the offer of Salvation is free. So, at MMH Bethany House the offer of the water of life (a symbol of God's Holy Spirit) was given to all who repented of their sin and accepted Christ as their Lord and Saviour.

(Incidentally, in a book '*The History of Louth*' – Louth being a town to the north of Boston – the writer records a Water Seller going around selling water!)

Fishers of Men

BETHANY HOUSE, as we decided to name 8 Pump Square, had at one time been a Fish Merchant's house. We too, as a Mission, were in the fishing business, fishing for the souls of men! The Lord Jesus called Simon Peter and Andrew:

> *Mark 1:17* "Come ye after Me, and I will make you to become FISHERS of MEN."

We would not only be going out to give the Gospel of Christ to the residents of six Mobile Home Parks in Boston; but also be giving out Gospel tracts to visitors to the famous Boston Market each Wednesday.

Bethany House facilities:

On the Ground Floor, looking out on Pump Square, was a **Meeting Room**: here the Gospel of Christ was preached on Sunday Evenings; on Tuesday evenings the Bible was expounded, with Prayer offered; on a Wednesday there was a Coffee Morning, and monthly on Thursday afternoons there was a Women's Meeting.

Behind the Meeting Room was an **Ancillary Room** with a Library of Evangelical Books. My friend Sinclair Abbot from Dundee very kindly sent me boxes of books; the late Mrs. Helena Wood had given books, and others also donated books. Here Mr. Gilbert Stevenson in later years spent some of his spare time assisting the Director in helping with the MMH accounts, and was a great help in other ways, too. At the rear were the **Director's Office** and an enclosed yard. On the first floor was a **Flat**, complete with kitchen, bathroom, toilet and bedroom; and going up the stairs was a **Double Bedroom** at the back. On the top floor was a **Large Room** extending across the whole width of the building, with windows looking out onto the Square.

New workers joining the Mission used the first and second floors for accommodation, and this accommodation was also occasionally used by others in need.

42   Edwin Pratt – How he came to know the Lord

Edwin lived on the Lea Mobile Home Park in Boston, in a twin-unit bungalow in the left-hand corner of the Park, and was contacted through MMH door-to-door evangelism, not long after his wife died in 1984 (?).

Edwin was an Anglo-Indian – I think that he probably left India in the 1948/49 period and came to England. This was time of the partitioning of India, with all its loss of life. I remember Laura Sanlon was with me that particular afternoon – she was on a 3 months Field Term from Belfast Bible College – and together we called on Mr. Pratt. It was a very cold and snowy day. He kindly invited us into his home for a Bible Study, and we had not long sat down before there was a knock at the door: it was the Jehovah's Witnesses. Fortunately, he did not invite them in. I read the Scriptures and explained the way of salvation through the shedding of Christ's precious blood upon the Cross of Calvary to redeem us, and reconcile us to God. Prayer was made, for a battle was going on for his eternal soul.

I told him that he would have to make up his mind, and that he needed to tell the J.W.s not to call any more. We prayed much at the Mission for his salvation, and that he would be delivered from false teachers. When he was next visited he told me that he had told the J.W.s not to call any more. Praise God!

Bible Studies continued and he came to personal faith in Christ at 80 years of age. When he came to move off the Park and to live in a Retirement Bungalow, I had regular Bible Study each Thursday afternoon with him. He became a great Bible student, and witnessed to his family. He would say to me, "Have you read *Isaiah Chapter 42* or *1 Timothy Chapter 2?*"

At first, he was reluctant at first to come to the Mission's Sunday night Gospel Service in Pump Square. Obviously, it would mark him out as a Christian. Also, it isn't easy at 80 years of age to change your habits. But he did come, and was generous in that he wanted to give sweets to everyone!

A couple of Edwin's personal comments:
"When you read the Bible, it hits you."
"When I am low I read the Bible, and it is a help and comfort to me."

He wanted to tell his brother Eric, with whom he had lost contact, that he was now following Christ. The area where they had lived became part of Pakistan. I wrote many letters on his behalf to the Salvation Army; to Jean Mullinger, a missionary in Pakistan, and others, sadly without any success, this being before the age of Computers and the Internet.

Interestingly, his father had been an Anglican Lay Reader in India, and he showed me a notebook with Scripture Sermon Outlines, which his father had preached, and which were very good. His father must have preached those messages 40-50 years before, and also had fellowship with the Medical Doctors of the Ludiana Fellowship. More wonderfully, his father's prayers for his son were answered. Thus, it appears that Edwin had had every opportunity to come to know the Lord in his earlier life – but didn't take it. However, the Lord is ever gracious, and gave Edwin a second chance to hear the Gospel of Christ and be Saved.

According to my friend, Rev. Geoffrey Stonier, the people at Ludhiana (an American Presbyterian work) had a great burden for World-Wide Revival in 1857, prior to the 1859 Revival in England, Scotland and Northern Ireland.

I met Edwin's charming daughter Beverley, and his lovely granddaughter, who was a real treasure, and both of whom he greatly loved. Unfortunately, he developed Cancer of the mouth (probably due to him having been a smoker in his earlier years) and had to go to St. George's Hospital, Lincoln, for treatment. He witnessed boldly to his newfound faith in Christ to patients and staff, so that when I visited him, he introduced me as his Pastor, and it was easy for me to give out copies of the "News Special" (a Christian Testimony paper) and to witness to Christ's Saving grace to other patients in the ward.

Sadly, in spite of chemo and radium therapy and all the medical attention, he died within a week, and went to be with Christ, which is far better. It was my privilege to conduct his funeral service at Boston Crematorium Chapel, with many of his family present.

(Laura Sanlon, mentioned near beginning of this chapter, was one of the Bible College students from Northern Ireland, who was spending a "Field Term" at the Mission in Boston – more about this work in the next chapter!)

Obituary

*(A brief extract from Pastor Hector Hall's tribute at the funeral of **Edwin Sidney Pratt** at Boston Crematorium Chapel on Friday 6th October.)*

It is a great privilege for me today to say a few words of tribute to my good friend, Edwin Pratt.

2 Corinthians 5:8 "We are confident, I say, and willing rather to be absent from the body, and to be present with the Lord."

He is with Christ!

Mr. Pratt's Faith in Christ

It commenced four years ago when he was 80 years of age, through the reading of the Bible in his own home. I visited him almost weekly for five years for Bible Study. He said in 1987:

"You came to my home and brought Christ to me... I get great comfort from the Bible... God has been good to me, and I appreciate your fellowship."

He loved his Lord who died for him and rose again. He loved the Hymn by Philip Doddridge:

> *O happy day, that fixed my choice,*
> *On Thee, my Saviour and my God...*
>
> *Happy day, Happy day,*
> *When Jesus washed my sins away.*

He came regularly to our Evening Service at Bethany Christian Centre, until ill health prevented him. He loved and studied the Word of God. Incidentally, his father was a preacher of the Gospel in India over 40 years ago: his father's prayers were answered.

**Please remember in prayer Beverly and Dave,
Ian, Daphne and family.**

43   Field Term Students from Belfast Bible College

I commenced an evangelistic outreach with the Gospel in early May each year on Mobile Home and Holiday Caravan Parks in Northern

Ireland. This was usually done during the day, with Meetings in the evening in Evangelical Churches and Missions. This was during the 1970s and 80s, but I continued doing this ministry till 2004. During the early period there were the so-called 'Troubles'; a little later saw the opening of the new building of the Belfast Bible College at Glenburn House, Dunmurry, on the outskirts of the City.

As a result of my deputation meetings with the students at the College, the MMH had the privilege of welcoming students as part of their Course, to spend a 'FIELD TERM' of two and a half months in Boston to gain practical experience in evangelism – on the ground, *in winter!*

IAN CLARK was the first such student to come, in *January 1984*. Our welcome message was thus:

"We are pleased to welcome Ian, a student at Belfast Bible College, who hails from Shropshire and who is spending his Field Term with the MMH. We pray that he may have a spiritually profitable time on the mobile home parks in Boston".

Ian was engaged in personal evangelism on the Mobile Home Parks; and in taking part in Gospel and other meetings in Bethany House. He also helped in practical ways in re-decorating the bedroom on the first floor of Bethany House.

Excerpt from Ian Clarke's Prayer Letter

"I praise God for a very enjoyable and profitable Field Term spent with The Mission to Mobile Homes in Boston, Lincolnshire. The work mainly involved visitation evangelism on the Mobile Home Parks in and around the town. Most of the people there have been unreached by any of the established Churches and there is a valuable work being done by Hector Hall and others.

The Mission have a new headquarters opening up soon in the centre of the town, so pray God will use it in His work there. The Lord taught me much about dependence on Him and how that it's only in His strength that we can ever hope to achieve anything. An added bonus was to stay in a Christian home and witness 'living by faith' at first hand. God honours those who honour Him (1 Samuel 2:30)."

LAURA SANLON came to us in *January 1985*, and Carolyn and Sharon greatly appreciated Laura's fellowship, as did many other young people.

Welcome Miss Laura Sanlon – report by **Sharon Hall**

"On the evening of 12th January 1985, a Welcome Meeting was held at Bethany House, the MMH Headquarters. As part of her Three-Year course at Belfast Bible College, Laura is spending a Field Term with the Mission, which we trust will be of mutual benefit to Laura and to the Mission.

After a time of worship in song Pastor Hector Hall invited Laura to give her testimony. She told of being brought up in a Christian home and at eight years of age she trusted Christ as her Saviour. After turning away from Christian things during her early teens, at nineteen Laura re-committed her life to Christ and later came to the point of full surrender to what the Lord had for her to do.

She then recounted how the Lord led her to Bible College, and to Belfast Bible College in particular, and how the Lord has continued to guide and supply her needs since stepping out in faith.

Hector Hall then gave Laura a promise from Joshua 1:5 and commended Laura to the Lord in prayer. He then challenged us from Joshua 24:15 to be serving Christ in this present day, like Laura. He also urged us to support our sister with our prayers and in practical hospitality...

Mr. Gilbert Stevenson closed the meeting in prayer and a time of informal fellowship was had over refreshments.

Field Term Report by **Laura Sanlon**

"As my Field Term with the Mission draws to an end, I can look back on it with thankfulness to the Lord for His blessings.

It has been a privilege to share in this work and to see the Lord's provision, especially in the Headquarters 'Bethany House': no doubt the Lord has great plans for its use in the future. All those involved in the Mission have experienced the presence and blessing of the Lord at weekly meetings held there. There have been many opportunities for door-to-door work on the mobile home parks, and Mr. Hall and I have witnessed the Holy Spirit working in a number of people's lives. We would ask your continued prayers, that they might realise their need of salvation.

One lesson the Lord has taught me here, is that we must be emptied of self before we can be used, and it is 'faithfulness' that counts in His service.

136

I would like to thank the Hall family for their hospitality and fellowship, and pray God will continue to bless them in this work."
"Thy work shall be rewarded, saith the LORD." *(Jeremiah 31:16)*

As well as being fully involved Gospel ministry on the Mobile Home Parks, Laura, like Ian, also helped in a practical way, by cataloguing the Mission's Book Library.

To bring things up to date...
Laura spent twenty-six years working as a Christian Missionary with U.F.M. in Spain and finishing in Barcelona, where she was engaged in Youth ministry with God's blessing. She is now, in 2018, undertaking a new ministry in Nairobi, Kenya.

She writes:
*"I have been invited by the Leadership at **Nairobi Chapel** to help them set up and Co-ordinate a Programme for the training of Young People (17-25) in Cross Cultural Mission. (September 2018)*

This is 'Reverse Mission' as I will be helping train people from the Global South in missions to serve overseas and even in the West. I will serve alongside the staff at this church and be under the leadership of Pastor Oscar."

We pray God's blessing on Laura as she embarks on this new chapter in her life with the Lord's promised help. "Lo I AM WITH YOU ALWAY, even unto the end of the world. Amen." *Matthew 28:20.*

PAUL JAMIESON joined us in *January 1986*, and the following is the contemporary report from the February-May 1986 Issue of FAITH AND VICTORY, the MMH Newsletter.

Paul Jamieson Welcome Meeting
On Saturday 4ᵗʰ January a Welcome Meeting was held for Mr. Paul Jamieson – for the last three years the Mission has had the pleasure of having students from Belfast Bible College spending their two-and-a-half months Field Term with us. As we met together the warmth of the atmosphere inside Bethany House contrasted with the snowy evening outside. After a time of praise Hector Hall, MMH Director, introduced Paul and extended the hand of fellowship.

Paul then gave his testimony, telling of how he could now see God's preserving mercies at work in his life up to the time when he put his trust in Christ. He then related how the Lord had led him to Bible College, confirming each step as he trusted Him, and some of the important lessons he has learnt in his one and a half years there.

Hector Hall concluded our time together by asking us to pray for Paul daily, and he brought a challenge from Acts 9:6 ("LORD, What wilt thou have me to do?" A.V.). God desires <u>us all</u> to be entirely consecrated to the Lord's service. Pastor D. Baker closed the meeting in prayer. Fellowship and refreshments followed.

> *Seek ye first not earthly pleasure*
> *Fading joy and failing treasure,*
> *But the love which knows no measure,*
> *Seek ye first.*

> *Seek the coming of His Kingdom;*
> *Seek the souls around to win them,*
> *Seek to Jesus Christ to bring them*
> *Seek this first.*

That report in '*Faith & Victory*' also included a report from Paul of his experiences of evangelism with MMH:

'No! Not today, thank you!'

"This was my introduction to evangelism. A lady, who thought she knew all that there was to know about religion, said a definite, "No"! Nevertheless, my colleague and I continued on around the rest of the homes on the Tattershall Park. We were encouraged when we met Mr. X., a Christian man who needs fellowship. We told him about 'Bethany House' and pray that he will come and join us as we worship God.

The second Park (Lea) that we visited was much more encouraging. We had conversations with people. One such conversation was with a retired circus clown who was anxious to share his stories of the circus, and we shared the beautiful stories of the Gospel. A fair exchange! We called to see Mr. P. (the elderly gentleman who has recently come to accept Christ as his Saviour). We were encouraged at his growth in the Lord. What a delight to see this dear man seeking to know more about the wonders of God's Word.

The third Park visited has, for me, been the most fruitful. We made contact with a Miss. L., a middle-aged lady in a backslidden condition. She talked quite openly about many things, but she has no peace. Please pray that He may restore unto her the Joy of her salvation! We also had an interesting chat with another man (who has been visited frequently by

Mr. Hall). He also was open and one could tell by the questions that he was asking that he was under conviction of his sins. Pray that he will accept Christ into his life.

These are just a few of the many people we have met and I urge you to continue in steadfast prayer for the work of 'The Mission to Mobile Homes' which can be very difficult and discouraging. Pray that Mr. Hall will be encouraged as he serves Christ in this work, and that he will see more fruit for his labours."

P. Jamieson.

Update... Our friend Paul Jamieson is now the Rev. Paul Jamieson, faithfully serving God as Minister of Hillhall Presbyterian Church, Lisburn, Northern Ireland, previously ministering in Christchurch, Dundonald.

The Sights of London
The Belfast Bible College Students didn't get many treats during their time with us, but each student did have a special day trip to London. In those days Elsey's Coaches of Gosberton ran a daily Coach Service from Boston to Kings Cross, where we boarded the Piccadilly Line underground train to Green Park: there we got off and crossed Green Park to Buckingham Palace. We didn't see Her Majesty the Queen but probably saw the Changing of the Guard, with photos taken. Then we would walk *via* Victoria Street to Parliament Square and the Houses of Parliament and the "Big Ben" tower, with more photos taken.

After that we would venture down Whitehall to Downing Street. In those days there would be only one lone Policeman on duty outside No. 10, the Prime Minister's famous residence. No Iron Gates and top security as it is today, with a number of Policemen on duty. We had our sandwiches and refreshments in the Park, so we would have arrived there at about 1:40 in the afternoon. On one occasion at around 2pm as we – with others – waited impatiently, the door of No. 10 opened and the chauffeur came out, followed by Mrs. Thatcher. He saw her into her limousine, and drove slowly to the corner with Whitehall: as the car stopped at the corner, Mrs. Margaret Thatcher, Prime Minister of Great Britain and Northern Ireland, gave us a personal wave of the hand and a broad smile, then the car sped off to the Houses of Parliament.

We need to pray for wisdom to be given to those in authority in Britain and Nations across the world. (1 Timothy 2:2)

44 Evangelism on Northern Ireland Caravan Parks
by Hector G Hall

The following is taken from a feature with the above title in 'Faith & Victory', the MMH magazine, for September – November 1991

On Wednesday 8th May at 9.30am, I met Mr. T. for the first time, standing at the iron door of the concealed Bloomfield Caravan Park. He was just waiting for the refuse men to empty his "Wheelie Bin". I explained the way of salvation through the cross and blood of Jesus.

Then I took the Ulster Bus to Bangor and then to Groomsport Caravan Park.

Good Contacts at Groomsport
"**Maisie**" sat in a deckchair, thankful to God for the sunshine and fresh air. She told me of her illness, and I told her of the Saviour. She said "I believe in God, but I have not yet accepted Him as my Saviour."

I replied, "Behold, now is the accepted time; behold, now is the day of salvation (*2 Corinthians 6:2*). Don't you think it is time that you did?"

She did not directly answer the question, but she did ask me to pray for her friend Carolyn, who is seriously ill in Hospital, needing a heart and lung replacement. I held her hand and prayed for Carolyn's healing, and for Maisie's salvation.

A young man was digging up turf, so I went over to him and said, "Good morning! I am an evangelist over from England encouraging young chaps like you to repent of your sins and put your trust in Christ, who died paying for your sins at Calvary, and who rose from the dead three days later." I gave him a *John 3:16* tract: he then requested one for his boss, who, he said, had started taking an interest in the Bible, and attending Gospel Meetings. A '*News Special*' was given to him, and I drew his attention to the testimony of a London Bus driver on the back page.

A lady also seen on a previous visit was given an S.G.M. '*Passport to Life*' tract.

A Polish man stopped his car outside the Post Office and offered me a lift into town. I gladly accepted, and gave him a tract at the start, telling him why I was in Northern Ireland. "Why couldn't God make men perfect without the need for forgiveness?" he asked. However, he wouldn't let me answer the question, and he got a little worked up – he had been five years in prison in Germany.

Eventually I replied something like this: "*Genesis chapter 1* tells us God created everything 'good'. *Chapter 3* tells us that Adam and Eve, our first parents, rebelled against God, and sin entered into the world. We inherit a sinful nature, and Jesus died for our sins at Calvary."

"You won't believe this, but my youngest daughter **Sharon**, is going as a missionary to Poland!" I told him.

God at Work at Helens Bay Caravan Park
On Thursday 9th May – a dull day with a little light drizzle – the owner of this Park saw me approach, and asked with a welcoming voice, "Are you on your yearly visit?" "Yes!" I answered.

A Backslider Restored!
In the centre of the Caravan Park stood an old-style motor caravan of a decade or two ago, with its rear door open for fresh air. Guarding it was a fierce-looking Alsatian on what looked like a loose lead – but it *was* tied, although I did not know it at the time! As I came nearer to it, it became very excited, until suddenly the owner came out. Actually, the dog was doing a good job guarding two-year-old **Rebekah**.

Before the Gospel message was explained he, **Chris**, revealed that he was a "born again" believer over from Dorset, and that Christ had healed his sick wife. He kindly invited me in to his small mobile home and told me his story. After this, I read *Acts 2:41-47*, and he admitted that he had not continued in the Apostle's doctrine, and had been slack about attending God's house. However, we prayed, and he asked the Lord's forgiveness. We then enjoyed most marvellous fellowship together over hot dogs, and our brother did not want me to leave. **Praise God!**

The top field at Helen's Bay is now a housing estate, and seven men were working on the foundations of a house. To **the foreman**, I said, "I have come to tell you that Christ is the only foundation on which to build your lives". He replied, with a smile, "You have certainly come at the right time." He was given a '*News Special*'.

Please **pray** for all these contacts!

A 2018 Reminiscence of Belfast Friends
In the will of God, I spent a week or ten days each year for over thirty years (excepting 1974) in BELFAST, doing Gospel outreach and follow-

up at Knocknagoney Park (Residential), Helens Bay (see the 1991 Report above), and Groomsport and Baloo (Residential Park.)

At Holywood I would usually call and see Gordon and Ian at their Sports Outfitter's Shop. (Rory McIlroy, the famous Ulster Golfer, bought his first Golf Blazer as a lad from their shop.) On arrival Gordon would put the kettle on for a welcome cup of tea. It was always good to have fellowship in our Lord Jesus Christ, and to get up to date with each other's news. Whilst in the shop other believers would come in from time to time, like another friend Bill Houston, an R.U.C. officer. I first met Bill at Knocknagoney Hall, where I was able to minister the Word and report on the Mission's work on a number of occasions.

At Helen's Bay I would call and see Ann's aunty Norah who was staying with her daughter Muriel and husband Leslie. She was very kind and gave me snacks. In 1972 – at the height of the "Troubles" – Norah and Uncle Jimmy her late husband gave me hospitality in their home in the Old Park area of the City. They belonged to the Ebenezer Gospel Hall. He was a milkman in this mixed district, but was highly respected by all.

On the opposite road, Mountview Street, I shall always remember seeing a lone BRITISH SOLDIER on guard duty. As I say, all on his own: with a powerful gun in his hand, but Oh so vulnerable – I did feel for him.

On another occasion David Maitland, also an R.U.C. officer, arranged a meeting with the Young People of The Martyrs Memorial Church. Uncle Jimmy kindly motored me there in good time, with my large Aldis Projector Box. I waited outside the church Hall, as there was nobody about. Then a man appeared and asked me, "Are you a Paisley man?" I waited a moment, then answered "I am Christ's man". A spiritual meeting followed, with prayerful interest in the MMH. A number of these young men later became Free Presbyterian ministers.

45   New Workers – George and Ann Stark

It was a pleasure to speak to the students of **Lebanon Missionary Bible College** (later named Northumberland Bible College) at Berwick-upon-Tweed on 31st May 1985. Their Missionary Meetings were always attended by all of the staff, as well as the students. Prior to the meeting on that occasion they kindly invited me to join them at their evening meal – a *hot curry* meal! A jug of water was on the table, and I made the mistake of drinking a full glass – so the meeting was spiritually alive, and the Guest Speaker was hot! The ministry of the Word and the Coloured

Slides presentation of "Evangelism Among Mobile Home People" went well.

As a result of that meeting George Stark and Ann Wilson, an engaged couple, felt challenged by the Lord to apply to the Mission for full-time service. They filled out Candidate's Forms and both met the Mission Council. George joined first and Anne joined after their marriage. George was concerned about his financial support, and I replied:

17th February 1986.

"I understand your obvious concern. However, your Dependence has got to be upon God. It is He who is going to supply all your needs in answer to believing prayer in the name of the Lord Jesus. We have found God to be Faithful to His promises: look to Him and trust Him. Bring your needs to Him in prayer, and He will surprise you yet."

Testimony and Call...

...Given at the **Welcome Meeting** at Bethany House on 15th March 1986. George read *Philippians 3* and gave his testimony and calling to the work of the Mission:

"My mother became a Christian in 1964. My father is not a Christian. I became a Christian at the age of eight. I felt the need of Christ in my life. There was a battle before I yielded my life to Christ.

An O.M.S. (Oriental Missionary Society) representative spoke at the ***Forth Gospel Mission*** *on Isaiah 6 and I was challenged to give myself to the Lord for full-time service and this led to Bible College.*

I was doing a survey of Missions in the U.K. Christian Handbook and noticed that the MMH had just two full-time workers – that stood out. When Mr. Hall came to the Lebanon Bible College and showed Coloured Slides of the Mission's work I felt challenged by the size of the work and the need to take the Gospel to people in mobile homes. The Lord also spoke to me at my Valedictory Service from Colossians 4:17 "Take heed to the ministry which thou hast received in the Lord, that thou fulfil it."

I would value your prayers."

George made himself at home in the first floor flat at Bethany House, did good outreach work on the Boston Mobile Home Parks, and cheerfully took part in all the activities of the Mission. He occasionally preached the Gospel service on a Lord's Day evening, and led the Tuesday night Prayer and Bible Study Meeting. He also attended the

Gospel Hall in Trinity Street, Boston, on a Lord's Day morning, and often came to us for dinner and tea.

Rev. B. E. Lambert gave the message at the **Welcome Meeting** at Bethany House for **Mr. George Stark and Miss Ann Wilson**, 15th March 1986. He first of all paid tribute to the faithful service of Pastor and Mrs. Hall, who had completed 25 years in full time Christian service with the Mission. He read *Luke 10*, with its message that *Jesus* sent them "Two and Two": Hector and Ann – and now George and Ann, and said he felt constrained to preach on neglected truths: The Sovereignty of God, Justification by Faith, and Revival. We need to have an exalted view of the Lord's work: you cannot improve upon the New Testament pattern. He then spoke on the *Lostness Of Man*, and asked the question "How FAR AWAY is Man from GOD??"

An enormous distance separates man from God – man is "far off" (*Ephesians 2:13*). Is it not a miracle, then, that we "are made nigh by the blood of Christ"? He referred to *Jonathan Edwards* who preached mightily against sin: "Sinners in the hands of an angry God". As he read this sermon by candlelight, people gripped their seats in fear, convicted by the Holy Spirit. They were attentive to the Word of God. There is *no such fear of God* or of impending judgement today. We have buried the doctrine of Hell. *Deuteronomy 32:35* "Their foot shall slide in due time: for the day of their calamity is at hand." "Where shall the feet of Christ rejecting sinners go?" the preacher asked. He spoke of the *everlasting misery* of the impenitent: *Deuteronomy 32:29* "Oh that they were wise, that they understood this, that they would consider their latter end!" Who cares about their end?

People are amassing wealth. We need a passport to Heaven: are *your* passports all in order? In *Luke 10*, the LORD appointed them (the Seventy). He sent them "two and two" (35 pairs). Notice the Harvest. The Harvest truly is great *v2*. It is time to be deadly serious. We are to throw out, cheap dishonouring methods. We are interested in God's register of those who are saved and those who are lost. It is the Father who gives them to the Son (see *John 6:37*). We are to judge righteous judgment (*John 7:24*).

Finally, Pastor Lambert asked the meeting to bear up George and Ann in prayer. You go "forth as lambs among wolves!" *Luke 10:3*.

Will You Be Going To Gypsies?
by George Stark

"Before I began with the MMH this was a question that I was asked while attending an after-Church Service for young people. This question amused me somewhat, but I at that time could only say 'No' – not envisaging what was to confront me within a fortnight of starting with the MMH!

Mr. Hall and I visited the Gypsies recently with the Gospel message, and we were confronted by various responses as we challenged different people. What surprised me was the number of children that were about on the site. Children who have probably never heard the Gospel before! And they need to, if they are ever going to respond to God's invitation.

Whilst we did come across some opposition – it was only to be expected – we also were encouraged by a Gypsy who had a text from the Bible displayed Hebrews 13:8 'JESUS CHRIST the same yesterday, and to day and for ever', shown for all to see on the window of his caravan. Enoch was his name, and he is a Christian with a considerable amount of knowledge of the Scriptures, but he has lacked the fellowship and teaching due to his absence from God's House.

Pray that he might be encouraged and stirred by the Holy Spirit to have Christian fellowship once again, and that he may continue to bear witness and indeed bear fruit among the other Gypsies after we have departed. Will I be going to Gypsies with the Gospel? My answer now would have to be YES!

It was a privilege and a joy for Ann and I to attend **George and Ann's wedding** in Glasgow on 20th July 1986. After their honeymoon they came to live in the flat that George occupied, now with additional rooms, at Bethany House. It was easier for George because he had in a measure settled in, since he had served in the Mission for four months prior to the wedding; but it would be true to say that Ann found it more difficult to settle in. It also had been the first year of their marriage. Ann helped with the Women's Meeting and the team outreach to Boston Market on a Wednesday morning. Ann's church, Hamilton Baptist Church, was very supportive of George and Ann.

George and Ann resigned in March, after George had completed one year with the Mission, in order to leave the Mission in April 1987. This was because they had applied to Africa Evangelical Fellowship (A.E.F.) for ministry in Africa. They had always had a Missionary interest, and served for a time in Malawi.

46 A Vacancy at Bethany House

THE MISSI **ILE HOMES.**

Tel. (0205)
351608
65689

Bethany House
8 Pump Square
Boston
Lincs. PE21 0PL

13th November I989

A Vacancy for 1 year Commencing 1ˢᵗ July 1990

The Mission has a Vacancy for a Christian person (or couple) to serve the Lord on a short-term appointment for one year, at our H.Q. in Boston.

Perhaps a Bible College student with a desire to gain further practical experience in preaching and visitation evangelism, before serving the Lord at home or overseas. Or it might suit an active retired couple who wish to be more actively involved in the work of God for 1 year. There is a flat available.

Please write to me giving details of your conversion, call to service, and details of your Christian service to date.

Yours sincerely,

Pastor Hector Hall, Director. (HGH/ACH)

After much prayer the above letter was composed and sent out to several Bible Colleges.

A couple who answered the letter were Noel and Sandra Ramsey, from Newtownabbey, Northern Ireland. Noel was shortly to finish his studies at Belfast Bible College, and had one year free before he could take up the Pastoral ministry at Eston Congregational Church, Middlesbrough.

Noel Ramsey's Testimony
"I was brought up in a good home but not a Christian home, and I was sent along to Sunday School and Boys' Brigade (B.B.) in a local Methodist Church but I never remember hearing the Gospel.

When I was 14 years of age our family moved house to outside Belfast. I had to change schools and in that new School a Christian befriended me, and eventually started to witness to me. Shortly after this my oldest brother became a Christian and I did see a change in his life. So I decided to go along to my friend's church and it was there that I heard the Gospel.

On 12th October 1975, during a Gospel Service God took to dealing with me and convicted me of my sin. I knew I needed to be saved, I knew Christ had died for me, so after the Service I spoke with the pastor, Rev. Tom Shaw, and I gave my life to the Lord. I then got involved in that Church and became a member of it. It is still the church of which I am a member today. The Church is Abbotts Cross Congregational.

As soon as I became a Christian I became involved in Youth Fellowship and another Christian Group called Young Life Campaign. I became a leader in the Youth Fellowship and the Youth Club. I was involved in door-to-door visitation evangelism with my church, and spent 5 years with U.B.M. (United Beach Missions) during Summer Holidays."

MMH Report for July 1990 by Noel Ramsey

We appreciated the ministry of Mr. Peter Assheton (MMH Chairman) at our Welcome Meeting, and his practical advice was carefully heeded. Most of our first week was spent unpacking our personal belongings and settling in to our new environment.

I made my first visit to Tattershall Lodge Mobile Home Park along with the Director. I found this visit informative as I observed how the Director approached each situation. Most people were friendly and a good conversation was had with a R. C. lady from Leeds who was visiting the Park.

As we visited the Lea Park on 17/7/1990, we had many good opportunities to share the Gospel with a number of people. It was encouraging to see God at work in Mrs. P's life, as she was reminded of the words that the Director had shared with her on previous visits.

On 19th and 20th the Witham Town site was visited. There was more opposition on this site to the Gospel.

However, good conversations were had with some who opposed our message. A good conversation with a lady called Christine; she has four children and she was very interested in sending them to a Children's Club if one could be organised. There were a number of children on this site, and I believe that a Children's Club for one week in August should be tried.

I was introduced to those who live on the Holland Park by the Director, and again literature was given out to a number of people, and a word for Christ was spoken.

The most profitable visits I had came when I revisited the Lea Park. It was obvious that God had been preparing hearts. Mr. Akitt invited me in and I had a good opportunity to share Christ with him over a cup of tea, although our time was cut short because his daughter came to visit him. Mr. Walter Elsey also invited me in and asked me to share with him how I got involved in Christian work. It was a good opportunity to give my testimony and before I left I read from *Hebrews 12:12-16*.

On my first visit Mr. Warner had refused to take a booklet but, on this occasion, he was willing to listen and accepted a booklet.

All these people need prayer and I trust that God will water His Word as it is planted in men's hearts.

I have had the opportunity to do some visitation around the local area, inviting people to the services at MMH Bethany Christian Centre: most people were friendly, but they tended to be reluctant to talk about "spiritual matters". The following streets were visited: Pump Square; Main Ridge West; Pen Street, Botolph Street, Grove Street, Threadneedle Street and Tawney Street.

Our Team Outreach to the famous Boston Market was very worthwhile, as many '*Way of Peace*' tracts were given out and we trust that God will use these for His glory.

The services at Bethany House have been well attended and God has been blessing His word. The attendance at the Wednesday Coffee Morning has been disappointing with only a few people coming, in spite of the busyness of the Market Place. In conclusion the past month has helped us to learn more about the work of the MMH, and has given us many opportunities to share the GOSPEL of CHRIST. We look forward to many more opportunities in the future.

For three months of that year (1990), from early September to the end of November, Hector and Ann were in Guelph, Ontario, CANADA. This time was spent in evangelising and in endeavouring to form a Council of suitable Canadian Pastors and others. This was in order to prepare for the *Incorporation* of the Mission work in Canada – more information later on that subject.

Upon our return to Boston, I asked Noel for a brief article for our *'Faith & Victory'* newsletter. Unfortunately, I cannot find that article, but fortunately the apt title is remembered: "BUSINESS as USUAL"! The instructions that had been left were faithfully followed. Gilbert Stevenson saw to the day-to-day financial matters; Carolyn our eldest daughter attended to matters at home, and Noel and Sandra were in Bethany House, with Noel faithfully involved in the ministry of the Word and Gospel – his faithful discharge of those duties being with his wife Sandra's support. Noel was of course also involved with outreach to the Parks, and the arrangements worked very well.

All of Noel's monthly reports for the whole year with the Mission were excellent, showing consistent Gospel outreach and follow-up. As he himself wrote:

"I wish to express thanks to God for all his grace through the past year and for the many opportunities He gave me to share the Gospel to needy people."

At the end of his year with the MMH, we received his letter:

8 Pump Square,
Boston, Lincs.
PE21 6QW

22nd May 1991

Dear Council Members,

I wish to tender my resignation from the Mission to Mobile Homes as from 30th June 1991.

May I take this opportunity to thank you all for your support throughout the past year. It has been a privilege serving the Lord with the Mission and we trust that God will continue to bless the work in the future.

Yours in His service,

(Signed) Noel Ramsey

Noel, Sandra, Jason, and their new baby girl went on to Eston, Middlesbrough, where Noel became minister of the Congregational Church, with our blessing and prayers. He is now Pastor of Wensleydale Evangelical Church, High Street, Leyburn, North Yorkshire.

47   John and Margaret Bugg

JOHN joined the Mission in June 1988 as an evangelist for DEVON and the South West. Whilst John was in the public eye, so to speak, Margaret served faithfully in the background in bringing up their three children, Rebekah, John Junior and Sarah, and, like Ann Hall, wife of the Director, in providing a good loving home base and prayer support. John was of a quiet demeanour. He could and did preach, but personal evangelism was his particular gift. He was and is of cheerful countenance and served faithfully for twelve years, from 1988 to 2000, the longest serving fellow-worker apart from the Director. He also served as an MMH Council Member.

He was used of the Lord to open up a <u>new area of Gospel Outreach</u> for the MMH in the southwest of England, beginning with the residents of DEVON Mobile Home Parks and Holiday Caravan Parks. He was initially based at Dartmouth (where the *Mayflower*, the Pilgrim Fathers' ship, docked *en route* for Boston, Massachusetts, U.S.A.) and later was based in Totnes.

You may well wonder why I am writing this report of John's work with MMH, and not John himself. Well, John sadly now has dementia, and is no longer able to do so. When I did ask John for his report after he had left the Mission, he replied that he had cleared out his papers on moving to Totnes, which was a pity. However, I am endeavouring to do justice in recording his ministry – as far as possible – in using his own words, taken from his articles and reports in *Faith & Victory*, the MMH Newsletter. Needless to say, I have had to be selective in so doing. As mentioned, John served on the Mission Council, for seven years, giving a report each year of His Gospel work on Devon and other south-western Sites at the MMH Annual Meetings, and contributing to the MMH Conferences.

We also arranged for Mr. Patrick Grace (who with his wife Ursula had served in LAOS with O.M.F.) to give John support. He did this well, as did Pastor West, minister of Dawlish Baptist Church. John would meet up with Patrick *en route* to MMH Council Meetings, and they enjoyed fellowship and friendship.

John Bugg's Testimony

"I became a Christian in 1960. God brought me under a deep conviction of sin through reading the book 'Peace With God' by Billy

Graham, also through his preaching on Closed Circuit TV in a local Methodist Church. I made a public commitment of my life to the Lord in the City Temple (Elim) under the ministry of Rev. Green.

Since then my desire for GOD has been a constant factor in my life. Prayer, Bible Study and study being vital, I benefited greatly from reading Christian books. I have had a desire to share the faith ever since."

John's letter of application to the Mission:

Dear Pastor Hall,   *Dartmouth, Devon,*
                                                      7th December 1987.

Greetings in the name of our Lord and Saviour, JESUS CHRIST.

I am writing in reply to your advert for a full time Christian worker with the Mission.

As you will see from my CV, I worked with C.C.A. Mission* for Home Evangelism (in a full time capacity) for nine years in total – seven years in the city of Hull (Kay a young teenager saved, and Mr. & Mrs. G., an elderly couple, brought to faith in Christ through the 'Three Score Years And Then' tract, and then linked up with an Evangelical Church where they heard the Gospel preached), then for two years here in Devon, living in Totnes. I continued selling Bibles and Christian literature as a Colporteur.

Since leaving C.C.A. three years ago, the jobs at the Royal Naval College, Dartmouth, (as Steward and kitchen assistant) and at Battarbees Ltd (hardware sales assistant) have been very fulfilling jobs whilst 'marking time' and seeking what the Lord wanted us to do next!

I would like again to be actively involved in home-evangelism.
                          Yours in Him,
                          John Bugg

(* C.C.A. – Christian Colportage Association, now Outreach UK)

From the MMH "Faith & Victory" Newsletter, July-September 1988:

NEW EVANGELIST FOR S.W. AREA.

The Commissioning service on 11th June of Mr. John Bugg could have been a dreadful let-down! A 500-mile round trip from Leicester to Dartmouth and then – no one to commission. Mr. Bugg had been taken ill and was confined to bed. But in the goodness of God it was no such thing. A small but very warm fellowship welcomed us on a beautiful day and we knew that God's hand was upon us in blessing in spite of the adverse circumstances.

We *did* have a service, which was taped for Mr. Bugg, led by the Pastor of the Church, Pastor Norman Allnutt. He spoke of Mr. Bugg's call and assured us of the Church's total commitment to him in the work of the Mission. Pastor Hector Hall (Director of the Mission) preached from *Mark 16 verse 15* "Go ye into all the world, and preach the Gospel to every creature", and related this to the work of the Mission, the needs of the people in Mobile Homes, and John's call.

We were invited to tea following the meeting, and had a good time of fellowship. We were sorry to leave new friends made.

Three of us went to see Mr. Bugg in his home before returning home. He was still in bed, but beginning to feel better and rejoicing in God's healing hand. We had prayer before leaving – a precious moment.

Please remember Mr. Bugg, his wife and three teenage children in your prayers. The field is white, the labourers are few – but God is faithful.

Betty Hayden.

From the MMH "Faith & Victory" Newsletter,
October-November 1988:

MY CALL TO THE MISSION
By John Bugg

Calling on God
My 'Calling' goes back a long way, when in my early twenties I heard God calling me to repentance and faith in the Cross work of Jesus.

It was a joyous day when I in turn called on the Name of the Lord and experienced His great Salvation (*Romans 10:13*).

Calling on People
Even as a "Babe in Christ" (*1 Corinthians 3:1*), I realised that those who needed to hear the Gospel were mainly outside the four walls of the "Church". There was given to me an earnest desire to reach out by visiting

door-to-door around the local Methodist Church to share this "Good News". Doing this and then later working full-time (for nine years) in Home Visitation confirmed, to me, the tremendous value of this form of Evangelism.

God's New Call

After this time of great activity for Him, the Lord took us through a "Wilderness Experience". It was late in 1987, when, looking on a daily basis at the "Situations Vacant" columns, I spotted an advert for MMH in the "Christian Herald", saying that they were wanting new workers. So, in early December, I wrote off for an Application Form, etc., and after an exchange of letters, went to see the MMH Council.

In April 1988, after much consideration and prayer, both Margaret and I went up to Leicester to meet the Council.

The Council were encouraged in the response of Prayer Partners to the idea of our joining the Mission, and so the Invitation was extended to us. Margaret and I, being similarly convinced that it was right to take this step of faith, were happy to accept.

"For whosoever shall call upon the name of the Lord shall be saved."
Romans 10:13

Evangelism on Devon Mobile Home Parks

"Every place that the sole of your foot shall tread upon, that have I given unto you... I will not fail thee, nor forsake thee... This book of the law shall not depart out of thy mouth... do according to all that is written therein... be not afraid, neither be thou dismayed: for the Lord thy God is with thee whithersoever thou goest." (*From Joshua 1:1-9*, A.V.)

I felt very much as Joshua must have done, as he was about to lead the Israelites into the Promised Land. But these words of God to him are an encouragement to me in setting out in mainly strange territory as I begin my work with the Mission to Mobile Homes in the South West.

My first task was to find out where the Parks were! People, Telephone Directories and books in the library gave this information. My next task was to see whether it was possible to get to any using the local means of public transport (i.e. buses, trains, boats).

As the difficulty of getting to all residential parks without a car was recognised, my visiting brief was extended to include Holiday Parks as well.

So far, Praise God, the following Parks have been visited:

Residential Caravan Parks:

Stoke Fleming:	Deer Park
Paignton:	Ayreville Park
	Beechdown Park
	Himalaya Park
Goodrington:	Goodrington Orchard
Plymouth:	Glenholt Park

Holiday Caravan Parks:

Dartmouth:	Little Cotton
	Norton Park
Goodrington:	Holimarine Park
Brixham:	Sharkham Point Caravan Park
	South Bay Holiday Village

There is a need to be especially prayerful in approaching the Managers of the Parks when seeking permission to visit. The Deer Park manager refused Hector and I permission to visit. Yet on another occasion, a member of staff said I could. On a third visit a different member of staff (known to me), obviously briefed, again refused. Having already made contact with some folks on the Park, I was able to visit them, so I also posted Christian literature through the letterboxes at the same time.

Holiday Parks are a different proposition to the Residential Parks, as these managers are often afraid that by allowing "religious visitors" they might lose trade. In all of this we need to be "wise as serpents, and harmless as doves" (*Matthew 10:16 A.V.*).

So much for the general picture: let us now "Zoom In" and look at a particular Park. I have found the folks on Beechdown Park (near Paignton) very open and friendly. Here are details of some people spoken to on this large Park (of about 100 homes).

On a second visit to this Park, a young lady invited me in and offered me a cup of tea (being joined by her husband). I learned that she belonged to the Brixham Methodist Church, and was keen for her husband to go also, and HAVE FAITH!

Next door but one I spoke to a lady very taken up with the teaching of an Indian Guru… On a later visit she expressed a desire to go to a local "live" Church. As transport was a difficulty, I contacted the Pastor.

At another home, I was invited in by a middle-aged man with a strong Birmingham accent, who had moved to Devon to enjoy a slower pace of life. He was obviously a "thinking man", but keen to point out the bad side of "religion". I sought to make him realize that the Creator would one day be our Judge, and that we would all be accountable on a personal basis on that day. Then I explained how we can be accepted in Christ in spite of our sinful nature! I gave him a copy of the booklet "*Consider Jesus*" (S.G.M.).

Please make the following a matter of Prayer and Praise!
And PRAY…
- That God will open a door for our message
- That we may proclaim it as clearly as we should
- That we may be wise in the way that we act toward outsiders, and make the most of every opportunity.

John Bugg

Great Is Thy Faithfulness!

We rejoice with John Bugg in the Lord's provision of a large gift, which has enabled him to purchase a good Escort Estate (T-Registered) car, and to pay for the insurance. We thank the anonymous donor.

Isle of Wight Outreach
23rd April – 7th May 1994

It was with a keen sense of anticipation that I set out in the car to go to the I. of W. for this fortnight's visitation on the residential mobile home parks. At Lymington, I met up with Michael O'Brien, a Christian friend from Hull, who was teaming up with me for the outreach.

We then crossed over to the Island on the car ferry. From Yarmouth we drove straight to Niton, and after unpacking, were soon settled in at The Bothy (self-catering accommodation kindly provided by David and Angela Cook.) The only visiting previously done by myself was a little on the Medina Park, East Cowes in 1991 and 1992 whilst over for the Keswick Week.

Our plan was to visit Medina Park, East Cowes, the largest Park with about 220 homes; Waverley Park, also at East Cowes with about 25 homes; Riverview Park, Newport, 4 homes (with concrete bases down for a further 12 homes) and Fernhill Park, Wootton, Ryde, with about 26 homes.

People met initially on the Medina Park were particularly unreceptive due to intense visiting done earlier by 'so called J.W.s'. Also, there seemed to be an unusual hardness in some women spoken to. Here and there, however, we had the conviction that God was at work in the hearts of individuals as we sought to share the Gospel. In the deputation meetings we stressed the emphasis placed on seeking to speak on the doorstep of the finished work of Christ on the Cross. Also, to give the wider picture of the M.M.H. ministry.

The Lord blessed us with mainly fine weather and certainly good fellowship with Christians met during the visit. A big thank you to all those that made this fortnight possible, (not least of all the two Margarets, our wives left behind!)

PRAISE GOD for: -

> Literature given out
> Opportunities for conversations
> Travelling mercies.
> Prayer and practical support

PRAY for:

- Man who thought it more important to be happy here and now than to face up to eternal issues.
- Lady whose grandson recently had a kidney transplant. She expressed sorrow that someone had to die in order that he might live. This gave opening to speak of Christ dying to give eternal life.
- Man in his middle 30's who couldn't read or write and never had a job. Able to speak with him of the love of God and the Gospel.
- Lady (in her 40's) who seemed to be listening intently. Sunday School and church background. Given a John's Gospel to read.
- Warden on the Park – only been there for two or three weeks. He had a very genuine concern about the violence etc. in today's world.

John Bugg (Devon)

John & Margaret Bugg, Dartmouth, Devon
Summer 1994

Overcoming the Opposition

My wife and I set out for Honiton, arriving at the Otter Valley Park early morning. We were a little apprehensive due to opposition and hardness previously met in the visitation there, yet confident there had been much prayer for this outreach.

This outreach was different in various ways. For one thing, we would be living on the Park for our time in Honiton. This was due to the kindness of Ruth Poulter in lending us her lovely home there! (Visiting previously on the Park, I had been told in no uncertain manner, 'We don't want strangers visiting here'. This could hardly be said of someone living there!!)

Also, there was to be a different strategy in the visiting. People were to be visited who had responded well when met in previous years. Also those who Ruth told us might appreciate my calling. But the final plan as to who to visit was decided after speaking with a Christian couple living on the Park.

The keynote, then, of the visiting was to be selective (in military terms – precision bombing!).

Please pray especially for: -

- Mr. G. – a Mormon who didn't see that my evangelical faith was very much different to his! His wife, who recently had a second heart attack, and the family are all Mormons.
- A couple – that the Bible notes passed on will be instrumental in them both coming to a saving faith in Christ.
- Mr. E. told me 'I am not an atheist'. Had to explain to him, that on the basis of his rejection of God's Word that he was not a Christian! (My sheep hear My voice.) Gospel leaflet taken.

It was good on the Sunday to go along to the Honiton Congregational Church in the morning and then in the evening to the Meadow Vale Chapel (Open Brethren) to have fellowship with local Christians. Also to go along on the Tuesday evening to the Honiton Congregational Church to show a set of slides of the work of the MMH and to report on the visiting done on the Otter Valley Park to date. (We were encouraged in

157

the prayer interest shown). Pray that we and the local Christians will have an increasing burden for lost souls!

Psalm 126:5-6 (A.V.) "They that sow in tears shall reap in joy.

He that goeth forth and weepeth, bearing precious seed, shall doubtless come again with rejoicing, bringing his sheaves with him."

John Bugg (Devon)

Devon Parks to be visited next:
   Pathfinder Village, Tedburn St. Mary
   Beechdown Park, near Paignton
   New Park, near Bovey Tracey
   Katerleat Park, Ashburton
   Ashburton Caravan Park
   Cat & Fiddle Park, Clyst St. Mary
   Firs Park, Exeter
   Ayreville Park, near Paignton
   Newport Park, Topsham, Exeter

The Mission to Mobile Homes
Summer 2000

Report of Outreach in the Weymouth Area
8th - 15th May 2000

John Bugg – The Mission to Mobile Homes

Mobile Home Parks Visited:
1. Weston Caravan Park, Portland
2. Handborough Park, Chickerell, Weymouth
3. Rowlands Caravan Park, Chickerell, Weymouth
4. Cerne Villa Park, Chickerell, Weymouth
5. Montevideo Park, Chickerell, Weymouth

It was an encouraging time visiting on the Parks, with some good conversations and opportunities to pass on Gospel literature, etc. On the Thursday I was joined in the visiting by Tim Serjeant of Home Evangelism, who lives in Wyke Regis.

These are just some of the people spoken to – please pray for: -

G., a devout Roman Catholic, getting over a stroke - felt a great love and affinity for him. Able to speak with him of the 'finished work of Christ'.

A man belonging to the Church of England - a 'professor' but not, I think, a 'professor of faith', with whom I had a long conversation. He told me that he did not usually speak to people like me on the doorstep!

Another man sat on a bench outside his home on a really hot day, glad to talk to someone (he lost his wife seven years ago.) He told me that he prayed, so I said, "That's good to talk to God", and suggested that he read his Bible and allow God to speak to him. Bible notes to help him were declined.

A man, 93 years old, had doubts as to whether God is the Creator, or that Jesus was born of a virgin. Able to share the Gospel.

A lady, M., still in her dressing gown, was reluctant to talk, thinking I was a member of a cult, but her whole attitude changed when she realized that I was a Christian. An invitation was given me to go to her 'Baptist' church on the Sunday.

A., a mild-mannered man, turned out to be a Jehovah's Witness. He willingly accepted my Gospel leaflet without wanting to pass on his literature to me!! Shared with him some proofs of the Holy Spirit's personality - e.g. how is it possible to grieve, or lie to, etc., an active power?

It was good to have fellowship with Christians in the local churches, showing slides of the work and talking about the visiting in the Weymouth area, at Ebenezer Evangelical Church on the Wednesday evening, and also going along to the Chickerell Gospel Hall on the Sunday evening, and meeting people previously only spoken to on the phone.

I was saddened to see that a Mormon Temple is being built at Chickerell to be completed in December 2000 at a cost, I am told, of one million pounds! It is important that we are very much in prayer about this, and that individual Christians in the area are equipped to deal with the smart young men who will soon be knocking on their doors!! The 'Reachout Trust' seeks to help Christians combat the onslaught from Cult members.

It was a great joy to be able to go into HM Prison – The Verne, Portland – with Arthur Thurston, on the Saturday morning for the weekly

Bible Study that he leads on the Kairos wing. I was able to share about the work of the 'Mission' and the visiting in the Weymouth area. The Christian men there had such a love for the scriptures and were so keen to learn more.

IN CONCLUSION

John, I believe, became a little weary in well doing (*see Galatians 6:9*) after twelve faithful years of sowing the seed of God's Word, and didn't see much outward response to his ministry. Only those who labour in this type of ministry know what is involved. The Lord alone knows the whole picture.

However, we need to await the verdict of eternity when all will be revealed.

We rest in the promise
Isaiah 55:11 "So shall My Word be that goeth forth out of My mouth: it shall not return unto Me void (i.e. empty), but it shall accomplish that which I shall please, and it shall PROSPER in the thing whereto I send it."

Nonetheless, the Lord in his goodness has allowed their three children to come to saving faith in Christ: Rebekah while they were in Hull, and John Junior and Sarah while in Devon. Ann and I are still in touch with John and Margaret and pray regularly for the family.

H.G.H.

48 God at Work Among the Gypsies

In the early days of the Mission while we were at Moulton, Northampton (1968?) I reached out with the Gospel of Christ and came to a little residential Mobile Home Park in Burton Latimer, a village famous for its Weetabix Factory. On this park, in the right-hand corner, was a small four berth Caravan with a Gypsy family as residents (the only Gypsy family on that site) – Edna, Jack, Shane and a baby girl. Their mobile home was spotless.

They warmly welcomed me in and I read the Scriptures and prayed with them, and they gave me a cup of tea. In time I got to know the whole wider family in the Thrapston area. They all heard the Gospel. Ann arranged some special Children's meetings. They were not well advertised or attended, but a good time was had with the children, teaching them Bible Stories and Christian choruses. Jack did Tarmacadam work, and as they prospered they bought land and had a house built. Shane their son was a bright lad and went to Kettering Grammar School.

Many years later, probably in the early 1980s when we were in Boston, Shane who by then had married Dolly from Newark, called at Beulah, our home, to tell Ann (as I was away in Belfast at the time) that he had come to know the Lord as his personal Saviour, and what's more, his mum Edna and his dad Jack had also come to know the Saviour. What a wonderful encouragement, what a wonderful answer to many prayers. To God be all the Glory for the great things He has done!

> *Ecclesiastes 11:1* "Cast thy bread upon the waters, for thou shalt find it after many days."

'Wee Shughie'   **Lanarkshire, Scotland – April 1979**

We at last found Heathery Knowe Traveller's Park, after touring round most of Coatbridge. Across the field the horses roamed, nibbling the grass. Mrs. Hall stayed in the car praying as I went forth in weakness, but the Lord undertook. Each caravan was visited, and I told the Easter message to the occupants. Three young people in one caravan listened to the Gospel of Christ who died for our sins upon the cross of Calvary, and rose again from the dead the third day. A *'Gospel of St. John'* was given to the eldest girl to read to her brothers and sisters. Copies of the *'Emergency Post'* were handed out to all. Two men received tracts, but were more interested in doing business over the sale of a car.

A little lad followed me round, he wanted a *'Gospel of St. John'*, so I said, "Wait until I have visited every home, then if there is one left in my case you can have it." After visiting the last few homes, we met a man who said He was not interested. "God is interested in you; He sent His Son to Calvary to die for your sins: repent and get right with God, I replied. As he was eating his sandwich rolls, it being lunch time, I left him to think over the message.

The little lad was still with me at the end. He told me his name was 'SHUGHIE'. He did get his copy of the Gospel, and its message was explained to him. It appears that he goes to school in Townhead, and had heard the Message of the Cross from a minister who had visited his School. Please pray for this lad's conversion.

H.G.H.

Children's Mission on Boston Gypsy Park
3rd – 7th August 1987
Contemporary Report by Ann C. Hall

GOD works when we step out in faith and let Him work through us. For a number of years, we have felt the need to reach the Children on the Gypsy Site.

When Sharon came home from the Bible College of Wales, Swansea, for the summer she felt that God wanted her to do a **Holiday Club** on the Gypsy Site in Boston.

One afternoon in July 1987 Hector and Sharon went around the Park taking the Gospel and seeing how many Children were on the Park. On 5th August Sharon set forth in fear, knowing that she was not going in her own strength but that God was with her. We have had opposition on the Park at other times but much prayer went before her. The Lord worked wonderfully. The average attendance was about fourteen (one day there were seventeen), the age range being from a few months to thirteen years. Hector and I were there as the back-up team.

We had a time of prayer before we set forth each afternoon, and we saw the Lord answering the prayers that we prayed about the weather – we were spending an hour each afternoon sitting on a rug on a spare piece of grass on the park and it didn't rain during the time we spent with the children. (Clouds appeared but no rain, praise God!)

We taught them some choruses, but at first, they couldn't sing, so we made this a matter of prayer. One girl asked, "Can we sing 'He made the stars to shine'". The girl sitting next to her said, "How do you know that – you weren't here yesterday?", but she told her that one of the other girls had been singing it during the morning and thus she had learnt it. By the end of the week they were singing quite happily as they coloured their pictures.

We had **three of the Mums** come over to see us on Wednesday afternoon wanting to know where we were from; what were we teaching them – and were we Catholics, as they were Catholics? We answered their questions: "We are Bible Believing Christians from The Mission to Mobile Homes, Pump Square." We wondered if they would stop their children coming, but they were there the next day and the next.

Sharon faithfully told the children about JESUS and HIS LOVE, and how HE DIED on THE CROSS and ROSE AGAIN. Also, how they

162

needed to be sorry for the naughty things in their lives, how they could ask JESUS into their hearts, and how He would help them day by day. The Ice-Cream van turned up one afternoon and they spontaneously bought ice creams for their younger brothers and sisters.

Finally, pray for these young lives, that the seed of God's word may take root. We don't know – there may be a future '*Gypsy Smith*' from this group!

Ann C. Hall

49   First Known Canadian Convert
Martins Grove Park, Waterloo, Ontario

In 1990 Ann and I went to Guelph, Ontario, Canada for three months (from early September till the end of November), among other things to see about the Mission being ***Incorporated*** in Canada, with its own Board (Council). Roy and Helene very kindly gave us the use of their basement flat at no cost to ourselves. The weather was hot and sunny at the beginning, but snowy and cold at the end of this period. The initial good weather enabled me to do new outreach on some of the Mobile Home Parks in reach of Guelph, and that had not been not visited before.

Melonie Legg
On previous visits (since October 1980) I had visited Mobile Home Parks, bringing the Gospel of Christ to numerous people, and following them up. One such contact was **Melonie Legg**, who was a Jehovah's Witness. I told her that Jesus Christ is the eternal Son of God; that Christ had paid for her Sons on Calvary's Cross, and that she needed to repent and put her trust in Him. A number of calls were made to her home.

Then one day Keith Lapsley was with me when we called on her, and Melonie said, "I believe that Jesus Christ is the Son of God and I have accepted Him as my Saviour". What a joy and encouragement that was to me, and also to Keith.

Later still I visited the Park and met up with Melonie, her mother, and Laura Grominsky and had good fellowship with them. Laura started a Sunday School in her home and Melonie and Tony's children went along. She did a good work among the children, teaching Bible Stories, memory verses, and choruses. On this occasion Melonie mentioned that she had cancer. She quoted *Psalm 118:17* "I shall not die, but live, and declare the works of the LORD". I read *2 Corinthians 2* and prayed with them.

Melonie said to me, "You were the first person to speak to me of my need of Christ as my Saviour: you always remember the first person who does that!". What an encouragement to me. She was full of the joy of the Lord. Sadly, the Lord in His wisdom didn't choose to heal Melonie, and she died as He wanted her in heaven. My heart went out in prayer to Tony and the children.

Melonie's mother, an ex-J.W., had also come to know the Lord, and she told me that she had attended a Conference in America recently where 1,000 ex-Jehovah's Witnesses had attended. It is amazing what God is doing – to Him be all the glory.

Mr. and Mrs. Lorne Martin

I must tell you of one other couple on this Park: Mr. and Mrs. Lorne Martin, an elderly couple. On the side of their mobile home next to the letterbox was *Ephesians 2.8* "By grace are ye saved through faith". Thus, the post person and everybody else received this Message.

Each time I called they welcomed me in, and always gave me a cup of tea and a sandwich. They attended Kitchener Baptist Church. Such hospitality is always a blessing when you travel a long way in the Lord's service. I was thus able to tell the people that I had come over 3,000 miles to tell them GOD LOVES YOU.

Sadly, on my last visit to them a '*For Sale*' sign was on their home. I knocked and dear Mrs. Martin came to the door to say her husband Lorne had died, and she was moving nearer to her daughter's home in Kitchener. I expressed my deepest sympathy. What a bright witness they had been for Christ over many years. We thank God for every remembrance of His servants.

The basement flat mentioned at the beginning of this chapter had limited facilities for cooking (a three-ring stove), so during the week we had dinner at an eating place in the Shopping Mall: that had everything, and was well heated in the Winter period. Occasionally on a Sunday we had a meal upstairs with Roy and Helene which we appreciated – at other time we managed.

Nearby, passing under the motorway via the tunnel, and just a ten-minute walk away, we discovered a true bit of Canadian Forest. There we found a running stream where we were able to relax, and enjoy God's wonderful Creation. On the way to and from there we passed a flock of geese – yes, *Canada* Geese! We have them in Boston – it can't be the same flock, but maybe they are related!

Canadian law at this time required that it was necessary for a mission working in Canada to have a **Canadian Incorporation**, and to have a Canadian Council. In order to achieve this, and to further the Gospel work, we had suitable Canadian Council Members ready to take office. However, the first attempt to establish this Mission failed: Ottawa is very pro-Roman Catholic. But our biggest problem was that an evangelist, with suitable leadership gifts and a real burden for the Mobile Home and Trailer Bark people, was sadly not forthcoming.

We were booked to fly home to England near the end of November 1990 with the Worldways Canada airline, but a couple of weeks before our departure date they ceased their operations! We contacted Stephen Walker Travel in Boston, U.K., and Mr. Walker arranged for us to travel on 27th November – just one day later than our planned departure – on a Charter flight, and at no extra cost! Praise God!

It had been good having Ann, my wife, with me on this adventure. Ann's legs were swollen because her doctor hadn't prescribed water tablets for her heart condition. Otherwise, praise God, we both kept well the whole time we were in Canada. Space forbids more reporting except to thank Roy and Helene for their fellowship and help; for the warm fellowship of people in the Canadian Churches, and those who prayed at home. *We look forward to a further harvest of souls on the Ontario Mobile Home and Trailer Parks, for God's Glory.*

50   Concluding Items

A.   Tribute to MMH Council Members

Proverbs 1:7 "The fear of the LORD is the beginning of knowledge: but fools despise wisdom and instruction."

PETER C. ASSHETON

A fellow member at Hoddesdon Baptist Church, and a lawyer by profession, Peter served the Lord as a Council member with rare distinction over the whole period of its history from 1968-2004. He was our Council Chairman for 31 years.

Getting the MMH officially recognised as a Registered Charity with the Charity Commission and keeping the Mission up-to-date with all the regulations over the years was part of his brief. His contribution was invaluable: his courteous and wise counsel was much appreciated, as was his fellowship.

The MMH had only two Honorary Treasurers in 36 years, namely Mr. H. Peter Rawlings and Mr. Donald G. Hayden. (Although in the latter years, following the homecall of Mr. D. G. Hayden, Mr. Gilbert Stevenson assisted the Director with financial matters at Headquarters, with the blessing of the Mission Council).

PETER RAWLINGS

Peter was at the inaugural meeting of the MMH Council at Kings Cross Baptist Church Hall, London, on Friday 13th September 1968; he was, and is, an evangelical Anglican, and a banker by profession. He was patient and understanding. He served with due prayerful diligence for the early years of the Mission i.e. from 1968 to 1979, and was a great help. He was an appreciated speaker at the 8th Annual Meeting in 1976.

DONALD G. HAYDEN

Don was a Chief Careers Officer for the city of Leicester when he joined the Council in April 1975, and was a very great help to the Mission. He was a cheerful, understanding man and he was, as you would expect, very good at interviewing Candidates for the Mission, and soon set them at ease: he was also good at chairing Conference meetings.

He bore his last illness, suffering from cancer, with quiet courage, and even then kept the Mission's books right up-to-date. That shows the integrity and faithful Christian witness of Don, ably and lovingly supported by his wife Bette and daughter Sally.

NIGEL T. BARBER

A most outstanding Council member; he had the necessary spiritual qualities but in addition brought a wider vision, since he at that time regularly travelled abroad with his work as an electrical engineer.

Nigel came to know the Lord in Norfolk as a teenager through the ministry of Tom Moore from Belfast, who had, many years before, trained with Ann's father William I. Creighton at the Missionary Training Colony in Norwood, South London.

For quite a number of years Nigel did a great job in helping me with the MMH *'Faith & Victory'* Newsletter. I prepared the copy for the press and he then computerised the copy for the Printer. He did an excellent job, each quarter. Needless to say, he couldn't do this without the loving support of his wife Anne. For anything of a technical nature, Nigel was the man. He installed the 'Menvier' safety system in Bethany House, the MMH Headquarters.

PATRICK GRACE

Patrick also served on The Mission Council for a number of years. He had been a fellow-student with Hector at the Bible Training Institute, Glasgow, now the International Christian College (I.C.C.), and had served faithfully with his wife Ursula with O.M.F. in LAOS.

He was gracious in nature as in name, and was a great help to our brother John Bugg, the Mission evangelist in the West Country, who was based in Devon. He was a great help because he had Missionary experience, and gave excellent Ministry of the Word, and being of Irish origin was a most acceptable speaker (he was of course a Cambridge graduate – but not required on Boat Race day!)

ANN C. HALL

As wife of Hector, Ann was the only female member of the Council. She served the Lord and the Mission to Mobile Homes very faithfully over the whole period of the Mission. She came from a Missionary family, and therefore had wide experience.

Ann joined the Council in 1973, where her main contribution was as minute Secretary, however she was also able to bring a woman's point of view on certain matters as required. For a brief period she had to forego her Minute Secretary role due to her serious heart condition.

In addition, she ran a Coffee Morning at Bethany House for 20 years, and gave helpful spiritual advice based on the Scriptures to many women who sought it. She also led the fortnightly Women's Fellowship, ably assisted by Mrs. Joy Ford*, our pianist. Being much given to hospitality: even after she had a pace-maker fitted, she was keen to continue her service for the Lord. On top of it all she brought up her family.

As the writer of Proverbs says:

> *Proverbs 31:30* "A woman that feareth the Lord, she shall be praised."

(* Joy's husband Stephen preached occasionally at the Mission, and was later called to the pastoral ministry while a member at Bethel Baptist

Church, Billinghay. He is now minister of Lordshill Baptist Church, Snailbeach, Shropshire.)

GEOFFREY J. STONIER

From the Evangelical Free Church, Welwyn Garden City, Geoffrey faithfully served for 12 years from 1983 to 1995. He was also the Guest Speaker at two MMH Annual Meetings. He and his wife Joy brought people to the Mission's Conferences, and generally helped further the work of the Mission.

He has of more recent years been led of God to found 'Preacher's Help', training Pastors in Biblical teaching in what is often called the Third World. The Lord is blessing the work in Mozambique, Nigeria and India.

ANDREW BOULTER

After becoming a Council member in July 1996, Andrew became Council Chairman in May 1998, as Peter Assheton, who had served so faithfully as chairman, felt that a younger man should be appointed. Peter still continued on the Council. Andrew had been always very supportive, and was a member of Reynard Way Evangelical Church, Northampton, (F.I.E.C.) where a number of our Annual Meetings were held and their fellowship and hospitality appreciated.

JOHN HUTCHISON

Pastor of the Free Methodist Church, Glengormley, Northern Ireland, John assisted me in deputation ministry in Ulster. (He had been pastor of Nazeing Congregational Church in my home village, and Hoddesdon Baptist Church, my home church). He and Marjorie his wife had in earlier years been missionaries in North Africa.

OTHER COUNCIL MEMBERS

Wilfred E. Boggis; Brian Morphew; John Dopson; Bernard Lambert; Gareth James, and last but not least, John Bugg.

B.   A Tribute to Faithful MMH Co-Workers

J. NEVILLE KNOX

I especially wish to place on record the support that our late esteemed president gave to the MMH. Although he was the Chief Executive of the great northern Municipal Borough of Harrogate, he spoke at four of our

168

Annual Meetings over the years. He was also the main speaker at our Residential Conference at the Christian Guest House, Sutton-on-Sea, Lincolnshire, on 2nd – 4th May 1986. The Theme was AMBASSADORS FOR JESUS CHRIST. He preached with liberty on the Lord's Day in the morning and afternoon at the adjoining Sutton-On-Sea Evangelical Church.

(Pastor Brian Keen of Whittlesey Baptist Church also gave excellent ministry of the Word from *2 Corinthians Chapter 5* on the Saturday.)

I don't know much about Mr. Knox's earlier life, but it was while he was stationed on the Isle of Islay during the Second World War that a verse of a hymn was used to lead him to faith in Christ:

> *Room for pleasure Room for business,*
> *But for Christ the Crucified*
> *Not a place that He can enter*
> *In the life for whom He died.*

He went regularly, almost every year, to preach in the Churches of Islay, where my father-in-law Rev. William (and Helen) Creighton was Pastor of Bowmore and Port Ellen (and Colonsay) Baptist Churches. I myself preached once in Colonsay Baptist Church. Mr. Knox was a capable lawyer and mixed with people in authority: he was bold for Christ and the Bible and not afraid to own his Lord, but conversely, he was humble and enjoyed fellowship of GOD's true people, whatever their social background.

When people complained about the weather He loved to quote the Psalmist:
> *Psalm 118:24* "This is the day which the Lord hath made; we will rejoice and be glad in it."

Every Christmas he always sent Ann and I a letter of encouragement, and assured us of his prayers and support.

NORTHERN IRELAND

Honorary Belfast MMH Representatives 1970 onwards:

Tom and Irene Meaney

David and Molly Maitland

Robert and Heather Bryce

Dennis and Pat Glass

They were all a great help to me, giving me gracious hospitality, fellowship and friendship particularly during the so called 'troubles'.

ADDED TO THEM:

Leslie and Margaret Lees

Relatives of Ann's, who usually gave me an Evening Meal on each of my visits, and Leslie kindly motored me to the Church or Mission meetings afterwards, sometimes in a difficult area of the City.

Mr. Philip Meachem

My fellow-worker in the Gospel who has done good outreach work on a number of Mobile Home Parks in the West Midlands (and also among Lorry Drivers). He has seen Sheila come to faith in Christ, on the Beacon Park, Walsall. He will no doubt in time tell his full story.

Jersey and Guernsey Christians

The evangelical Churches and Missions of Jersey and Guernsey in the Channel Islands have been an encouragement to the Mission over the years.

One of our faithful prayer-partners and friends Ruth Berry is now 109 years of age. We send Ruth our Hearty Congratulations. God is good!
Deuteronomy 33:25 "As thy days, so shall thy strength be."

C. In Conclusion…

I have yet more testimony to tell of God's Great Faithfulness, Mercy and Grace!

- How God provided different cars.
- Of Outreach on M.H. Parks in Florida, U.S.A.
- Of a Preaching Tour of Evangelical Churches in Naples and Southern Italy.
- Of a memorable visit to the Holy Land.

Perhaps a shorter book another time (if the Lord spares me), after a good rest.

Although the Mission officially closed on 31st December 2004, it has been my privilege to continue to preach the Glorious Gospel of Christ my Redeemer in evangelical Churches and Missions, and in following up people on the Mobile Home Parks and Holiday Caravan Parks mainly near to our home in Boston, Lincolnshire. I have been preaching for over 60 years.

As well as giving due care to my dear wife Ann. She had a serious stroke 2½ years ago (on top of her heart trouble) but endeavours to keep active in mind and body, serving the Lord.

A special *"THANK YOU"* to our faithful Prayer-Partners.

THE MISSION TO MOBILE HOMES
The Mission's Gospel Outreach, by Hector G. Hall at the Call of God, began across Central Scotland in June 1967. The Mission was officially constituted on 13ᵗʰ September 1968.

MMH ANNUAL MEETINGS – GUEST SPEAKERS

1969 Mr. Duncan Black

1970 Pastor B.E. Lambert

1971 Mr. Peter Assheton

1972 Rev. W. Rose

1973 Rev. G. Harry Sutton

1974 Pastor Derek Anderson

1975 Mr. J. Neville Knox

1976 Mr. H. Peter Rawlings

1977 Rev. R. B. Larter

1978 Mr. Cyril Lockwood

1979 Rev. G. Harry Sutton

1980 Rev. Barry Shucksmith

1981 Rev. J. T. Orrell

1982 Rev. Ronald Evans

1983 No Annual Meeting*

1984 Mr. J. Neville Knox

1985 Rev. Geoffrey Stonier

1986 Rev. Donald Densham

1987 Mr. Ron Smith (Fishers Fellowship)

1988 Rev. J. McClatchey

1989 Mr. J. Neville Knox

1990 Rev. Geoffrey Stonier

1991 Mr. Patrick Grace

1992 Rev. Gareth James

1993 Rev. Bob Sanders

1994 Mr. P. C. Assheton

1995 Rev. David Bugden

1996 Rev. George Hill

1997 Rev. Paul Mallard

1998 Rev. Paul Bassett

1999 Rev. J. McClatchey

2000 Rev. David Bugden

2001 Rev. Paul Bassett

2002 Rev. Paul Mallard

2003 Rev. Gareth James

2004 No Annual Meeting

* 1983 – No Meeting because we had just taken over 8 Pump Square, Boston, as H.Q.

D. Reasons for the Closure of the Mission

Prior to, and after, John Bugg leaving the Mission in 2000, we had a period of lost momentum. Patrick Grace also left around the same time as John, and there were no full-time workers appearing on the scene. Don Hayden had passed on to his eternal reward, and no new members had been added to the Council recently. J. Neville Knox, our esteemed President, had also been called home to Glory.

What brought things to a head was my reaching 65 years of age and possible retirement. However, I carried on after retirement age in the hope of a new Director being appointed for the Mission, but in spite of much prayer (and fasting), advertising and the Council diligently considering possible candidates, no suitable person appeared on the scene. The Council, after a lot of very serious consideration, reluctantly concluded that it was God's will that the Mission should close on 31st December 2004.

Hector, together with Ann, had served 37½ years continuously, without any sabbaticals. The meetings at Bethany House had continued, but numbers were considerably reduced.

I found it hard to accept, as it had been my life-time work. However, Counsellors drew my attention to:

> *Proverbs 11:14* "Where no counsel is, the people fall: but in multitude of counsellors there is safety." (i.e. wisdom.)

The Mission Council proposed that the proceeds from the sale of Bethany House should be used to secure a good Retirement Pension for the Director. However, I did not feel happy about this generous proposition. Ann and I had lived by faith in God to supply our every need, and wished to continue that way. After a lot of thought and prayer I suggested to the Council that the proceeds from the sale of the property, after all necessary expenses had been paid, should be equally distributed among five Missionary Societies.

So, it was unanimously agreed by the MMH Council who, after much prayer and consideration, took the decision to sell Bethany House to the highest bidder, as required by the Charity Commission.

BENEFICIARYS of the Sale of BETHANY HOUSE
It was a sad day when Bethany House, the Mission's H.Q., had to close its doors for the last time. Many had attended Mission Services over the 23 years since it opened, and had heard the glorious Gospel of Christ, listened to Bible ministry, been given Christian literature, or received counsel or comfort when in distress. Others had enjoyed Christian fellowship, and many prayers had gone up, not only for people on the Mobile Home Parks in many places, but also for missionaries serving Christ across the world.

A few people with a serious need to get away for a few days rest and recuperation had stayed in the upstairs accommodation, with the Mission's blessing.

We had experienced some great evening meetings: to mention just one, the Rev. George Ashdown of the Protestant Alliance gave a fine Lecture on JOHN FOXE, Boston's most famous son. Foxe was the author of *"Acts and Monuments"*, widely known as *"Foxe's Book of Martyrs"*, and with non-Christians attending there was much discussion following the meeting.

However, the MMH Council wisely – I believe – did respect my decision with respect to the beneficiaries.

WHO THEN were to benefit from the sale of Bethany House? I brought to the Council a list of five Evangelical Charities for their consideration.   After prayer they unanimously accepted the whole list.

In alphabetical order:

1. Fellowship for Evangelizing Britain's Villages.
Our brother Gilbert Stevenson, who had assisted the Director in doing the accounts for one afternoon a week for many years, without payment, and had attended many services at the Mission, had been an evangelistic worker with the F.E.B.V. in Suffolk in his earlier years. We also had fellowship with their workers and associated with them in the early days of the Mission, particularly in Essex, and with Braintree Evangelical Church (Arthur and Deena Little).

£22,471.42

2. International Christian College (I.C.C.), Glasgow.
This was another suitable recipient, as Pastor Hall had received his Bible and Theological Training at B.T.I., the forerunner of I.C.C.

£22,471.42

3. London City Mission (L.C.M.).
After completing the B.T.I. Theological Diploma course, Hector spent three years serving with the L.C.M., where Ann joined him after their marriage in June 1962. It was with L.C.M. that he learned, in effect as an apprentice, the ministry of Personal and Door-to-Door evangelism.

£22,471.44

4. Mission Africa (formerly Qua Iboe Fellowship).
David and Leon Griffith, veteran missionaries, served with this society, David being a fellow-student with Hector at B.T.I. They served very faithfully in Nigeria until David's wife Leon, a school teacher, was sadly killed. They were returning from a conference at night and drove into a vehicle parked on the road without lights. David was seriously injured. I visited him in the Queen Elizabeth Hospital, Birmingham. He had come with Leon to Bethany House to give illustrated talks on a number of occasions, when on furlough. Mission Africa is doing a great and expanding work today.

£22,471.42

5. Trinitarian Bible Society (T.B.S.)
T.B.S. Publishes the Authorised Version (King James) Bibles, New Testaments. and Scripture portions etc., that are sent across the World.

The most wonderful book that speaks of the most Wonderful Saviour, the Lord Jesus Christ.

£22,471.42

Total £112,357.12p

How this money was used by these Christian organizations – what God accomplished – may not be known this side of eternity. One prayer-partner later commented that EVERY PENNY had gone to Christian work.

May souls be saved and the Lord's great Name be glorified. Amen!

Redeemed, how I love to proclaim it!
Redeemed by the blood of the Lamb;
Redeemed through His infinite mercy,
His child, and forever, I am.
Chorus
Redeemed, redeemed,
Redeemed by the blood of the Lamb;
Redeemed, redeemed,
His child, and forever, I am.

I think of my blessed Redeemer,
I think of Him all the day long;
I sing, for I cannot be silent;
His love is the theme of my song.

I know there's a crown that is waiting
In yonder bright mansion for me,
And soon, with the spirits made perfect,
At home with the Lord I shall be.

Frances J. Van Alstyne 1820-1915

Appendix 1

The Mission to Mobile Homes – Doctrinal Basis

1. The full and verbal inspiration of all the Old Testament and New Testament Scriptures as originally given, and of these alone; their being in themselves the Word of God, without error, and wholly reliable in both fact and doctrine; their final authority and perpetual sufficiency in all matters of faith and practice.

2. The unity of the Godhead and the Divine co-equality of the Father, the Son, and the Holy Spirit; the sovereignty of God in creation, providence and redemption.

3. The total depravity of human nature in consequence of the fall, and the necessity for regeneration.

4. The true and proper Deity of our Lord Jesus Christ; His virgin birth; His real and perfect manhood; the authority of His teaching and the infallibility of all his utterances; His work of atonement for sinners of mankind by His substitutionary sufferings and death; His bodily resurrection, and His ascension into Heaven; and His present priestly intercession for His people at the right hand of the Father.

5. The justification of the sinner solely by faith in our Lord and Saviour Jesus Christ.

6. The work of the Holy Spirit as essential for a true and spiritual understanding of the Scriptures; for regeneration, conversion, and sanctification, and for ministry and worship.

7. The universal Church, the body of which Christ is the Head, embracing all the redeemed, called by God through the Gospel, born of the Spirit and justified by faith; the local church, comprising such believers, as the expression of the universal Church; and fellowship between such churches, manifesting the unity of the body of Christ.

8. The ordinances of Baptism and the Lord's Supper as being instituted by our Lord Jesus Christ, but not in Baptism as conveying regenerating grace, nor in the Lord's Supper as being a sacrifice for sin or involving any change in the substance of the bread and wine.

9. The personal return of the Lord Jesus Christ in glory.

10. The resurrection of the body; the judgement of the world by our Lord Jesus Christ, with the eternal blessedness of the righteous and the eternal punishment of the wicked.

Appendix 2

The Mission to Mobile Homes – First Prayer Letter

Prayer Letter

Morishill,
34 Dairy Road,
Beith,
Ayrshire.

June 1967

Dear Prayer Partners,

> *"Let us go up at once, and possess it;*
> *for we are well able to overcome it."*
> *Numbers 13.30*

Greetings in Christ's Name and many thanks for your prayers which have been abundantly answered.

It has been a growing conviction over the past few months that the Lord is calling me to evangelism among the 300,000 people living in Mobile Home Parks throughout the country. The Railway Mission kindly agreed to release me from 26th May: although I stayed on an extra week in order to bring the Office work up-to-date.

We praise our Heavenly Father for His blessing during the past three years:

1. Over 3,000 railwaymen contacted and given Christian literature on the Scottish Region

2. Re-opened Hall in Dundee, with virile nucleus of young people.

3. Conference.

4. New United Branches Youth Squashes. Souls saved.

5. New Area Rallies in Dundee and Kilmarnock.

6. Generous parting gift.

Please remember in your prayers the Scottish Committee that they know the Lord's guidance in matters of reorganization and

Messrs. A. Watt and J. Robertson in particular, as they carry on the office administration for the present.

MISSION TO MOBILE HOMES

As far as I know there is little coordinated evangelism among Mobile Home dwellers in Britain. The above figure (300,000) is the Consumer Council's estimate for 1965: probably the actual number of people living in residential Caravans in Britain today is in the region of ½ a million. Many of the Mobile Home Parks have 50, 100, 200 and even 300 vans and a large number are situated away from towns and villages. Where there are club premises or suitable buildings on the sites we shall endeavour to arrange a Sunday School, Bible Study group and even a Gospel Service on a Sunday.

On the Queen's Birthday Holiday (29th May) I visited the _Silver Sands Caravan Park at Lossiemouth_ on the Moray Firth: a gloriously hot day. I arrived late in the afternoon from Dundee and obtained permission from Major Hilary, the warden, to visit each of the 65 Mobile Homes and requested a caravan for the night. During the evening over a hundred people were contacted – door to door – each home received a copy of "The Evangelist" and children were given Scripture leaflets. Most of the men work at the Royal Naval Air Station (crews from that Station bombed the SS Torrey Canyon*).

A Baptist woman from Falmouth had been there a few weeks, but had not linked up with a Church ...a Church of England couple were contacted ...also a woman who said she "trusted in God", but did not see the need for prayer and Bible reading. At nearly the last home I met a young couple Bob and Margaret Weston. Bob lived for ten years at Stortford Rd, Hoddesdon – Hoddesdon friends take note! They invited me back for supper – answered prayer as I had nothing to drink and little to eat – and over the meal we discussed the way of salvation. Please pray that these dear people will be convicted of sin by the Holy Spirit and led to Christ.

178

Profitable visits have also been made at Clyde Caravans, Langbank and Bankfield, Ayr, where Jehovah's Witnesses were encountered, and many good contacts made. We hope to give a full report of visit to Langbank in MMH News Letter.

(* The 120,000-ton oil tanker SS Torrey Canyon struck a rock off the west of Cornwall in March 1967. The plan was to ignite the crude oil cargo from the air to prevent it washing up on the beaches.)

Cadet Hut Sunday School Football Team, rear of St Leonard's Rd., Nazeing *(Hector in the white shorts, 4th from the left)*

Bible Training Institute (B.T.I.) Glasgow – Staff & Students (1958-60)

The Opening of Bethany House, MMH Headquarters Pump Square, Boston (UK) Saturday 6th October 1984

JAM CLUB (Children's Mission)
Teacher – Sharon Hall

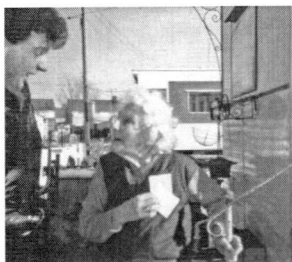

A Student from B.B.I. (N.I.)
witnessing on Lea Park, Boston

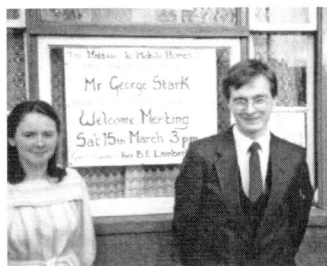

George & Ann Stark, MMH
Workers, at Bethany House

Coffee Morning at Bethany House, with Helena Wood, Laura
Sanlon, Ann Hall, Gilbert Stevenson, and Sharon Hall

MMH Conference at Hothorpe Hall, Leicester

MMH Council Members: Nigel Barber, Hector & Ann Hall, Pastor Bernard Lambert, Peter Assheton (Chairman), and Don Hayden
(See Chapter 50 for more details of MMH Council Members)

Personal Evangelism - MMH Director Hector Hall

John Bugg – witnessing on a Devon Mobile Home Park

Ann Hall giving a Flannelgraph
message on the Cross, at Boston
Gypsy Park

Adrian Underwood
MMH Leicester

Noel & Sandra Ramsey,
with Jason

After a Sunday
Evening Gospel
Meeting.
Mr Edwin Pratt is 3rd
from the right

Baptism of
Phyllis Flavell
by Pastor Brown at
Coningsby Baptist
Church

Dedication of the 1st
MMH Caravan Church
at Pentland Park,
Loanhead
15th May 1971
From the right:
Mr Angus, Rev C
Gellaitry (Portobello
Baptist Church)
Third from the left:
Mr A. Ritchie (Duns)
And friends from the
Park

James & Jean Brownlee

Sunday School Scholars
and Teachers